How to Talk to Your Kids About Drugs

Stephen Arterburn
AND Jim Burns

HARVEST HOUSE PUBLISHERS
EUGENE, OREGON

Jim Burns: Published in association with the literary agency of WordServe Literary Group, Ltd., 10152 S. Knoll Circle, Highlands Ranch, CO 80130

Stephen Arterburn: Published in association with the literary agency of WordServe Literary Group, Ltd., 10152 S. Knoll Circle, Highlands Ranch, CO 80130

Cover photo © Andrew Olney / Digital Vision / Getty Images

Backcover author photo for Stephen Arterburn © Lonnie Duka Photography

Cover by Terry Dugan Design, Minneapolis, Minnesota

HOW TO TALK TO YOUR KIDS ABOUT DRUGS
Updated, expanded edition of *Drug Proof Your Kids*
Copyright © 2007 by Stephen Arterburn and Jim Burns
Published by Harvest House Publishers
Eugene, Oregon 97402
www.harvesthousepublishers.com

Library of Congress Cataloging-in-Publication Data
Arterburn, Stephen, 1953-
    How to talk to your kids about drugs / Stephen Arterburn and Jim Burns.
    p. cm.
    ISBN-13: 978-0-7369-2010-0 (pbk.)
    ISBN-10: 0-7369-2010-2
    1. Teenagers—Drug use. 2. Teenagers—Alcohol use. 3. Teenagers—Counseling of.
4. Drug abuse—Prevention. 5. Alcoholism—Prevention. 6. Communication in the
family. I. Burns, Jim, 1953- II. Title.
    HV5824.Y68A784 2007
    613.80835—dc22

                                                            2006037382

Printed in the United States of America

07 08 09 10 11 12 13 14 15 / BP-SK / 12 11 10 9 8 7 6 5 4 3 2 1

To the most wonderful audiences of *New Life Live* and *HomeWord with Jim Burns*. We count it one of the great privileges of our life to share good news with you daily.

Special thanks to

Roger Marsh, for your research, friendship, and being the outstanding producer of the *HomeWord* broadcasts.

Cindy Ward, for your partnership in ministry and your dedication to making a difference in the world.

Roger Royster, for the great job you did with the Leader's Guide.

Jim Liebelt and Mary Perdue, for your friendship, dedication, and all you did with the *Drug-Proof Your Kids Kit*.

Contents

Preface

We wish we didn't have to write this book. We wish that not one child had to deal with the incredible pressure to try drugs and alcohol. Unfortunately, the overwhelming majority of kids you know and love will experiment with these substances. Worse yet, many of these kids and their families will suffer greatly from addiction and the other traumas that go along with substance abuse.

Far too many parents *assume* the monumental problem of drug abuse will never touch their children. Yet our experience tells us that no one is safe. We've seen thousands of kids—rich, poor, Christian, non-Christian, tall, short, high IQ, learning disabled, college graduates, fourth graders—seduced into drug and alcohol abuse. We've seen wonderful families caught totally by surprise and blown apart when drugs and alcohol became an awful reality in their midst.

This book contains a drug-proof plan we know works. A desperate mother came to us recently and said, "If I follow this plan, will you guarantee my children will be drug free?" We can't guarantee that every parent who reads this book will never see his or her children struggle with substance abuse. We can say that if parents follow the steps of this drug-proof plan, thousands of children will be spared the anguish of drug abuse. And while that's no guarantee, this book provides the best prevention measures you can take.

All studies show that if parents have good dialog and communication with their kids about drugs and alcohol use and abuse, those kids will be much less susceptible to experimenting with drugs. This book will give you the information you need to have that good communication with your kids. Remember: Kids learn best when *they* talk...not just when *you* talk. Find ways to dialog about these various subjects. It just might save you and them a great deal of heartache.

Our ministries, New Life and HomeWord, exist to serve you. If we can be of any help to you, don't hesitate to contact us. Our addresses are at the end of this book.

Be sure to check out the Study and Discussion Guide in the back of the book. In addition, a Drug-Proof Your Kids Small Group Kit, which includes a curriculum for youth groups, is also available directly from HomeWord.

A Proven Plan for Drug-Proofing Your Kids

Nicole can still remember the phone call. Janice was her closest friend, and judging by the tone of her voice, she was upset.

"You've got to come over!"

"Jan—what's wrong?"

"It's Emily. She's pretty messed up. You've got to get over here *now*, Nikki!"

A flurry of random thoughts flooded Nicole's mind while she sped over to Janice's house as fast as her SUV would legally get her there. Janice met her in the driveway, arms folded, head down, pacing.

"Where is she?"

"Probably still in the bathroom. She's been throwing up about every ten minutes since she got here. Ashley's with her right now."

"Is she sick?"

"It looks like she's *drunk*, Nikki."

"*Drunk?*" Nicole echoed. "That's impossible! She's only in seventh grade."

"Well, apparently Emily's become wise beyond her years," Janice responded. "In fact, I'm finding out things tonight about both our precious 13-year-old daughters that will make your head spin!"

Why Talk to Your Kids About Drugs?

Janice and Nicole learned a hard lesson that night about how easy it is for a couple of "good," "nice," church-going seventh graders to give in to the temptation to experiment with drugs and alcohol. The moms had a rather rude awakening to the severity of this subject. But *you* aren't going to go that route. What you're about to read will prepare you to talk to your kids about the dangers of drug use and abuse now. It will help you learn how to drug-proof your kids!

Drug-Proofing a New Generation

When we wrote the first edition of this book in 1988, we never dreamed it would have such a far-reaching influence and the incredible number of people who would read the drug-proof plan. Everywhere we have the privilege to share this drug-proofing message, people come up to us with their stories. It's often the story of a Christian family in which the parents had no idea their children were dabbling in the dangerous world of drug and alcohol abuse. Many of the stories are extremely pain filled and complicated. Most of the people tell us they were totally unaware of what to do about their family problem, and they wished they had come upon our material sooner. In 1988, we were fairly certain our plan worked. Today we can say *without a doubt* we know it works. We have seen positive, healthy, changed lives because families came together to work through the plan.

Along with the exciting "changed lives" stories, we've faced a major disappointment. Our experience has been that the majority of families *still* look at the drug and alcohol issues in our world as somebody else's problem. Instead of proactive parenting in this area, many parents still have a tendency to wait too long to get educated in the ways of prevention. One friend told us at the beginning of our work in drug and alcohol prevention, "The fastest way to empty an auditorium is to speak to parents about drugs and alcohol. No one thinks they have a problem until it's too late." Unfortunately, our friend was partially right.

Uninvolved Parents Raise Children at Risk

We remember a time when every parent in the large Newport/ Mesa, California, school district received a flyer describing a Red Ribbon Week—a school district-wide parents information night. The prospect of equipping thousands of adults to drug-proof the kids in their care was most encouraging. But on the night of the event, in a school district where thousands and thousands of students are enrolled in grades kindergarten through 12, *only three parents showed up!* Because we both live in this area, we know personally that hundreds of families in that school district suffer every year with the painful reality of drug and alcohol abuse.

We are inspired that you have chosen to rise above the norm in your efforts to learn how to talk to your kids about drugs and alcohol abuse. After reading this book, you'll have a better feel for the kinds of temptations your sons and daughters might be confronted with. You'll also have a basic understanding of the drug-proof plan. Your investment of time and learning will reap wonderful dividends in the future.

The Drug-Proof Concept

We have *not* based this plan on a quick fix or the latest fads. And, frankly, we haven't based this on the "Let's just wait for a miracle" approach. We based this plan on:

- The very latest in drug and alcohol abuse research
- Commonsense parenting principles
- Biblical values

We *can* drug-proof our kids. We *can* save them from the pressure to use drugs and help them take the steps to stop using them. The idea is comparable to weatherproofing a home. We cannot do away with the weather. The storms and floods will come. But the wise person has prepared his or her home to withstand the forces of nature so it will not be destroyed. Likewise, drugs are a present force. Alcohol is always available. But the drug-proof child will not be destroyed by them. At the end of the Sermon on the Mount, in Matthew 7:24-27, Jesus told the following parable:

> Therefore everyone who hears these words of mine and puts them into practice is like a wise man who built his house on the rock. The rain came down, the streams rose, and the winds blew and beat against that house; yet it did not fall, because it had its foundation on the rock. But everyone who hears these words of mine and does not put them into practice is like a foolish man who built his house on sand. The rain came down, the streams rose, and the winds blew and beat against that house, and it fell with a great crash.

Rain, wind, and storms will come into all our lives, but the wise family builds its foundation on the rock. Only the foolish assume sand is strong enough to withstand the storms of substance abuse in our world today.

The Benefits of Drug-Proofing

Drug-proof kids are given the chance to become whole, healthy, strong, and free human beings. Their parents lay the foundation for them to flourish. But it isn't easy. It takes great determination and a commitment of study, time, finances, and prayer. It requires following a plan through *every stage* of a child's life.

I (Steve) work with a man who had two sons go through a drug-treatment program. He determined his boys were in trouble, and he sought the best available help. He and his wife became deeply involved in the treatment process and were active in the long-term plan for recovery. He told me of their first Christmas together when both kids were off drugs and into recovery. He said it was the first time he felt like a truly free person—no longer a captive in his own house. The eggshells they had all walked on over the past years were swept out the door.

It's Never Too Early to Start

Drug-proofing can begin at any age. Kids about to enter kindergarten need to be prepared for people who have stooped so low as to pass off drugs as "magic pills" to small children. When my (Jim's) daughter was in kindergarten, at the age of five, she learned to say, "Hugs, not drugs." If a child has already experimented with drugs, it is still not too late. A child may be grown, have a family, and be a practicing alcoholic, but a parent can act to help free the child from addiction. It is *never* too late to become involved in helping a person who is abusing drugs or alcohol or both. There is always hope.

The key ingredient to a drug-proof plan is parents taking responsibility to help their children change. This duty cannot be delegated—not to the school, church, or anyone else. Besides, no one else has a parent's power to motivate a child to change. Drug-proof kids have hope mainly because their parents made a conscious decision to get involved.

Once you have accepted the responsibility to help your children, you are ready to form a plan and carry it out. Children involved with drugs and alcohol do not just wake up one day and decide to stop. They need all the help they can get, especially in the form of positive pressure from parents to change.

Immune and Invincible

Let's face it—most kids either think they are immune or they will exercise the experimental nature of adolescence and play with fire. But if you design and implement a comprehensive plan, you have an excellent chance that the children you love will be spared the destruction of drugs.

There are no shortcuts, no easy answers. Our plan and this book rely on three principles:

1. *God cares about families.* The Bible shows God's concern for families and spells out His principles for parenting. These set the standard for families to resist drugs and raise fulfilled and successful children.

2. *Common sense, genuine love, and good communication make a long-term difference.* "Train a child in the way he should go, and when he is old he will not turn from it" (Proverbs 22:6). Common sense tells us such training requires a plan. An important ingredient of the plan is strong communication with our children, motivated by a deep sense of love and concern.

3. *Always use the most effective drug and alcohol education, prevention, and treatment methods.* We have included in this drug-proof plan the best methods currently available. Sometimes people don't seek help simply because they don't know where to go or what to do. Some have even received critical misinformation. We encourage you to investigate all you can about "Public Enemy #1."

7 Points for Drug-Proofing Your Kids

The drug-proof plan involves the following areas.

Education

Parents must obtain the knowledge they need about drugs, alcohol, and addiction. The information must then be passed along to their kids. Unfortunately, this part of the plan is often neglected because parents assume their children already have the right information. Parents who gamble on others doing the educating are asking for trouble.

Prevention

Prevention involves rewards for responsible behavior and restrictions following irresponsible behavior. This is part of a good, overall parenting strategy that encourages kids to make right decisions and lets them immediately feel the consequences of poor choices.

Identification

When parents become aware that their children are using drugs or alcohol, the problem must be immediately evaluated. No such thing as "secret behavior" should be allowed. In this part of the plan, kids are not left to confront the problem on their own or work out how to get out of it by themselves. It is a family problem. If it is happening in the family, it must be known and dealt with by everyone. A part of the identification process is evaluating children's behavior so that if intervention is needed, it can be instituted as soon as possible.

Intervention

If the problem develops and is identified, this part of the plan allows for fast, appropriate, parental action to extinguish the undesirable behavior.

Treatment

Professional treatment comes in many forms, but if it is needed, nothing else can be substituted for it. An important part of the plan is you knowing what treatment resources are available and how to use them.

Supportive Follow-Up

This could also be called "relapse prevention." It enables the family to be part of the ongoing recovery process rather than to unknowingly destroy the foundations of lifetime sobriety. The entire family must be involved.

Self-Evaluation

Parents can't intervene effectively in the lives of their children unless the adults have made some positive decisions about their own involvement with alcohol and drugs. They may need to begin a recovery program themselves. Evaluation is also important for those who were raised in homes of a substance-abusing parent or who live with a substance-abusing spouse.

What the Drug-Proof Plan Is *Not*

The drug-proof plan is simple, comprehensive, and attainable if you are committed to saving your children. It is the best chance you and your family have to escape the heartache of addiction. However...

1. *The drug-proof plan is* not *based on quick fixes.* Like the heroin addict who must shoot up for a fast fix, our "instant soup, push-button mentality" always looks for the fast and easy way out. Drug and alcohol abuse are problems we can't put in a microwave for three minutes and be done with them. It takes time and effort. Quick fixes produce quick failures.

2. *The drug-proof plan is* not *based on new tricks.* People are always trying to provide a one-dimensional answer for this multidimensional problem. Almost every day, someone arrives on the scene with a new cure-all. But it soon fails because no single approach works. Beating drugs takes the coordination of several approaches and the cooperation of an entire family and/or community. Rather than new tricks, drug problems require old wisdom.

3. *The drug-proof plan is* not *based on* the idea *of "Let's wait for a miracle."* Doing nothing is irresponsible. Too many helpful resources are available for parents to sit back and leave the problem to work out by itself. False hopes have killed too many people.

One of my (Jim's) favorite stories in the Old Testament is the one about Joshua, Caleb, and the other ten spies who explored the promised land of Canaan (see Numbers 13). They found a land flowing "with milk and honey!" (verse 27), just as God had promised the Israelites when they were captives in Egypt. The spies reported the abundance and beauty of this land to Moses, but the ten spies also said emphatically, "We can't attack those people; they are stronger than we are" (verse 31). And the people of the community thought it would have been better to die in Egypt (see 14:2).

Joshua and Caleb, however, gave a minority report. Caleb said, "We should go up and take possession of the land, for we can certainly do it" (13:30).

What was the difference between the majority of the spies and Joshua and Caleb? They saw the same problems and opportunities. The majority said the situation was overwhelming. The minority stated that with God's help and a plan, they could face the enemy and succeed. History tells us Joshua and Caleb were right.

Dealing with the drugs at your doorstep can seem overwhelming. Like Joshua and Caleb, however, by seeking God's help and developing a plan, you can succeed.

THE SITUATION

Chapter 1

"Not My Kid!": Drug Abuse in Your Home

*I made good grades...was a small group leader
at church...and a cheerleader. My parents had no idea
that their 15-year-old honor student was an alcoholic.*

At the time Ashley's mother discovered Ashley's addiction to alcohol, her life appeared to be pretty normal. "My choice of friends was better than most. I came from a good Christian family. Everything looked great on the outside. My mom and dad didn't suspect at all that I had been getting drunk almost every day for the past two years. It's really kind of funny how you can be so deceptive to your own parents. I wanted their help, but I figured they wouldn't know what to say or do."

Is Ashley's story unusual? Hardly. The best of kids get entangled with drug and alcohol addiction, and their parents often have no idea of their kids' involvement—even kids who are involved in church. In fact, a majority of young people will experiment with drugs or alcohol.

The Numbers Don't Lie

Emily is 14 years old. She's an above-average student, very pretty, well-liked by her peers, faithful in attending church, and comes from a stable, middle-class home. Everyone believes Emily has a lot going for her. But by the time she graduates from high school, the chances are:

- 80 percent—she will experiment with alcohol[1]
- 53 percent—she will try an illicit drug[2]
- 49 percent—she will have tried marijuana[3]
- 32 percent—she will get drunk at least once[4]
- 21 percent—she will smoke marijuana regularly[5]
- 9 percent—she will try cocaine or crack[6]

And these are conservative estimates at best.

The Numbers Have Faces

The young people from whom these statistics are derived have names and faces. They come from every walk of life: rich and poor; liberal and conservative; Christian, Jewish, and Hindu; rural, suburban, and inner city. In twenty-first-century America, we have a growing drug problem from which no one is immune.

Every parent wants to believe his or her children will escape the epidemic of drug abuse and alcoholism that is daily engulfing millions of young people. Unfortunately, no matter where you live, your children have not escaped. You probably have hoped you would be able to do and say the right things to make them immune to temptation. You may have prayed, begged, and threatened in your attempts to keep the epidemic from touching your family. Yet we've heard what seems like thousands of anguished parents tell us, "We never dreamed it would happen to us."

Losing Larry

Larry was in my (Jim's) youth group at church. He was a fun-loving kid, and everybody liked him. But one day his parents sat in my office deeply grieving the loss of their only son. The night before, Larry went to a party, got drunk, and lost control of his car while speeding down a busy highway. Three kids were dead, and the driver of the other car was in critical condition. Apparently Larry was a teenage alcoholic. None of us knew until it was too late.

Larry's parents kept shaking their heads as we planned the funeral. They said, "We had no idea. We just assumed it would never happen to people like us. We suspected Larry drank periodically, but we thought it was harmless. Please tell other Christian parents—before it's too late—that their kids aren't safe just because they're involved in church activities."

Who's to Blame?

The actions taken to curb this mounting epidemic of drug and alcohol use and abuse can be summed up as "too little, too late." Neither the government nor the private sector has done enough to reduce the demand for drugs or to get them out of our schools, our neighborhoods, our communities, and our country. Each day, the epidemic robs us of lives that could have made a tremendous difference in this world. People who could run new companies, invent useful products, and care for the needy are destroyed daily. With the push of a needle, a snort up the nose, or a wild drive by an intoxicated kid, drugs steal our nation's future.

We are the most violent, crime-ridden country in the industrial world. This is partly because we are the biggest user of illegal drugs. We have 5 percent of the world's population and use 50 percent of the world's annual output of cocaine. And while our future shoots up, snorts, and overdoses, various committees, bureaucracies, and misguided people who are off on quick-fix tangents cripple the efforts needed to free our kids.

Why Too Little, Too Late?

Since the 1988 presidential campaign, both major political party platforms have identified drug abuse as one of the nation's biggest problems. Yet the government has not produced the results parents need, and it may never be able to cut off completely the supply of drugs. As governmental resolve and force increase, so do the resolve and force of those who profit from our children's addictions. No matter how hard we fight as a nation, those who run the drug trade will find a way to expand their markets and increase their profits. No, the government will not and cannot solve this problem.

We believe, however, that *together* we can drug-proof our young people. Hope lies in parents who will take action—one family, one neighborhood, one community at a time. Pointing fingers at the state capital or Washington, D.C., won't get the job done. Each parent must step back and answer the question, What can I do to save the children? Too few parents ever ask that question. Fewer still take action.

Let's look at four major reasons parents are not making the difference they could in this epidemic: *ignorance, denial, guilt,* and *fear.*

Ignorance Is Not Bliss

Even in the midst of massive publicity about the drug problem, many people *still* don't believe that drugs and alcohol are threats to *their* children. They hear the reports and read the statistics, but they rationalize that these stories involve faraway people in faraway places. They don't realize that no neighborhood has been left unscathed by this problem. As a result, when their own children get into trouble, parents are usually the last to learn about it.

We spend a great deal of our time training Christian workers to deal more effectively with youth and families, and we're always amazed at the ignorance found in the church. In a recent study on the church and substance abuse, 94 percent of the pastors and clergy members surveyed said they recognized drug abuse as a major problem among family members in their congregations. Yet only 36.5 percent reported that they addressed this issue at least once from the pulpit during the past 12 months—and 22.4 percent admitted they have never preached on it at all![7]

A Case Study

A while back, I (Steve) counseled a parent whose teenager was a full-blown alcoholic, a victim of the epidemic of abuse of one of the oldest known drugs. The girl's symptoms were clear, but her parents were totally ignorant of her condition.

I became involved through a call from the girl's youth pastor. She was in his office, and he didn't know what to do with her. When I arrived, it was apparent many tears had been shed that day. This beautiful, young girl and her youth pastor then helped me understand the nature of the problem.

High Tolerance

By the time he had picked her up that morning, she had consumed a pint of whiskey and half of a fifth of vodka. Now we're talking about a girl who might have weighed all of about 110 pounds, so the fact that she could consume so much alcohol was a clear signal she had a tolerance far surpassing that of most drinkers of the same weight. I asked if her friends had ever mentioned that her drinking was different from theirs. She admitted that on several occasions her friends had expressed deep concern about her drinking. They had pointed out that they got drunk on three or four drinks, but she could consume an entire bottle of hard liquor during the same time period and seemed hardly affected by it.

Tolerance plays a large role in the development of alcohol addiction. Most people who have alcoholic tendencies have to drink a great deal of alcohol to get addicted to it. This girl had a severe drinking problem that needed treatment. Hers was not a mild case or an example of an adolescent attempting to adjust to life. This was true addiction to a chemical—and her parents were blissfully unaware of the problem. They were Christians but so uninvolved in their daughter's life that they hadn't noticed she drank and thus had failed to see her progression into addiction. Their ignorance had left their daughter to fight her way out of the problem on her own. Fortunately, her fight began with a call to a youth pastor. Others are not so fortunate.

Dealing with Denial

It's always easier to deny the existence of a problem than to take action—at least initially. Denial takes many forms, but it's always used to avoid pain or to delay action. When the issue is drug or alcohol addiction involving one or more of their kids, some parents actually know what's going on but deny the seriousness of the problem.

We refuse to notice when our children develop a pattern of weekend illnesses that are manifestations of being hungover. We turn away at the sight of dilated pupils or drooping eyelids, excusing them as signs of a lack of rest. While the children form lifetime patterns of dependent behavior, the parents rationalize that what they see is a stage or a phase their kids will outgrow.

Parents in denial refuse to face their children's condition because they're unwilling to experience the temporary pain that comes when intervening in a person's life. Denial blocks out the need to act, allowing the drug problem to grow, the young addict to suffer, and the family to descend into dishonesty and farce, where everyone learns how *not* to deal with problems.

"Not in *My* Family!"

Another major concern leading to denial is the stigma that addiction brings to a family. The embarrassment of other people knowing that all is not well prevents parents from taking action. Saving the family's image is more important than doing what needs to be done.

Denial is deadly, however, and must be overcome. The stigma of a drug problem in the family is never as great as the pain of a death due to drug overdose or some other drug-related incident.

Are Christian parents immune from denial? Absolutely not. Because of a distorted view of spirituality, many Christian parents refuse to believe their kids might be involved in drugs or alcohol. They think their faith ensures that this plague can't contaminate their children. But no one is exempt.

Blaming Yourself for Your Child's Problem

Parents who feel guilty about their children's condition are often unable to act because they blame themselves for what their sons and daughters are going through. They play the "if only" game and always lose. Berating their methods of child rearing, they take on the weight of every poor decision made by their kids. They're unable to make tough, necessary decisions because they're paralyzed by guilt and remorse.

These parents are so wrapped up in their own problems that they don't see a clear path for their children, so they do what's easy. They encourage the kids to do better rather than demand the end of drug and alcohol use. Some parents allow their children to drink alcohol at home under the permissive battle cry, "If my child is going to drink, I prefer it be done under my roof." This dysfunctional philosophy comes from trying to compensate for past mistakes.

Guilt, the great paralyzer, stands in the way of rational thinking and parenting actions that produce change. It's a key reason we do too little, too late. Only when parents become aware that guilt sometimes keeps them from making the right decisions can they be free to help their children and not place undeserved blame on themselves.

Fear and Substance Abuse

My (Jim's) friend Sylvia's first marriage ended in tragedy, and her second marriage was a tragedy from the beginning. Her new husband was in the later stages of alcoholism and was violent and abusive. Sylvia became a textbook victim, and her children turned to experimenting with drugs and alcohol. She knew about her kids' problems but was afraid to confront them because, as she told me one afternoon, "If they also reject me, I have nothing left to live for."

Many parents, like Sylvia, don't react appropriately to drugs at their doorstep because they fear their children will reject them forever. Some fear what might lie ahead if their kids do change—the fear of the unknown. Others are afraid of doing the wrong thing and making the problem worse. Each fear becomes another excuse not to act, allowing the drug epidemic to continue. If kids are going to stop abusing chemicals, parents must move beyond their fears and into action.

Overcoming the Obstacles

We have to learn what's helpful and then do it. Ignorance, denial, guilt, and fear must be overcome by a tough kind of love. This is how you begin to drug-proof your kids and stop the growing epidemic.

Chapter 2

The Facts About Drug and Alcohol Abuse

A frantic mother called to tell me (Steve) she had found some suspicious things in her daughter's room. She didn't know what to do. I told her to bring the items to my office. She arrived about an hour later. The mother's hands shook as she laid each item on my desk: a small brown vial—it was empty, a capsule—also empty, a syringe, and a rubber tube. The final item was a glass pipe with some water drops condensed on the inside of its small globe.

The mother knew what lay before her—proof that her daughter was a drug abuser. She wept as she told of the times she had found other items that were all explained away by her daughter—a joint that "was placed in her pocket by mistake," a pill "she was just keeping for a friend who had a cold." This mother felt guilty for not seeking help sooner, for denying it could happen to her child.

Drugs Affect Every Family

As this woman learned so painfully and personally, society has become a victim of drug abuse and alcoholism in a way never seen before. And the problem continues to grow. Ask your kids about it. They'll tell you of kids who peddle new drug products out of school lockers or on neighborhood corners; of the kids who have started smoking cigarettes, moved on to marijuana, and then began inhaling the fumes from burning pieces of crack cocaine; of a society of kids who drink to get drunk with increasing frequency.

The Cost of Addictions

In October 2006, a report in *Forbes* magazine named alcohol, smoking, and drug abuse as the three "most expensive addictions" in the U.S. Total cost to us as a society: $433 billion a year—about $1,433 for every man, woman, and child in the nation. That might seem like good news because this number is actually lower than a generation ago. However, when you factor in a large increase in the population of the U.S. during that same time period, it actually represents an *increase* in that total cost.[1]

Alcoholism Leads the Way

Without question, the most expensive addiction is alcohol. It costs our nation $166 billion each year to replace what it takes away in lost wages, property damages, and medical costs. In fact, 25 to 40 percent of all Americans in general hospital beds are being treated for complications of alcoholism.[2]

As staggering as the numbers are, remember that they don't even begin to come near the incalculable emotional damage alcohol can do. Talk to those who've been raised by alcoholic parents, maimed by drunken drivers, or lost everything because of an alcohol problem. The answer to the question, "How bad is it?" is simple: Very.

Kids and Alcohol

How bad is the problem as it relates specifically to young people? The National Council on Alcoholism reports the following statistics:

- About 10.4 million Americans between ages 12 to 20 had at least one drink last month.
- In one survey, 30 percent of kids in fourth through sixth grades reported that they had received "a lot" of pressure from their classmates to drink beer.

- By the time they reach ninth grade, 56 percent of kids have tried alcohol. By their senior year, more than 8 out of 10 have taken their first drink.

- Alcohol-related highway deaths are the number one killer of 15- to 24-year-olds.

- An estimated 3.3 million drinkers ages 14 to 17 are showing signs they may develop serious alcohol-related problems.[3]

It's no surprise that kids are experimenting with alcohol at a much earlier age than a generation or two ago. Brewers and beer distributors are spending 15 to 20 million dollars a year to market their products to college campuses. Binge drinking is glamorized on MTV and the Internet, leading many teens and preteens to want to imitate this kind of behavior. Heavy drinking among students contributes to poor grades, vandalism, injuries, and death.

Talking to Your Kids About Alcoholism

Kids today are making decisions about alcohol and drugs when they are 10 to 12 years old. So if you've been wondering when to start talking to your kids about alcohol abuse, now is that time! The younger a person starts drinking, the more likely he or she is to develop alcohol-related problems later in life. Don't wait until your son or daughter has a problem with alcohol to address this crucial issue.

If you think your son or daughter is *not* affected by teen or preteen drinking, think again. Just because *they* are not the ones taking a drink doesn't mean they're not at risk because of some other kid who *did*.

- 56 percent of students in grades 5 through 12 say that alcohol advertising encourages them to drink.

- Middle school, junior high, and senior high students consume 1.1 billion beers annually.

- About 24 percent of the tenth graders and 32 percent of the twelfth graders in the United States say they have been drunk in the last month.

- Among teenagers who "binge drink" (consuming five or more drinks in a row on a single occasion), 39 percent say they drink alone, 58 percent drink when they are upset, 30 percent drink when they are bored, and 37 percent drink to feel high.

- Alcohol use is implicated in up to two-thirds of all date rapes and other sexual assault cases among teens and college students.

- 18 percent of high school girls said that it is acceptable for a boy to force a girl to have sex with him if she is already drunk or stoned (39 percent of high school boys agree with that statement).

- Almost 80 percent of teenagers don't know that a 12-ounce can of beer has the same amount of alcohol content as a shot of whiskey.

- 55 percent of teenagers don't know that a 5-ounce glass of wine has the same amount of alcohol content as a can of beer.[4]

In spite of the best intentions of many parents to caution their kids about the dangers of alcoholism, the fact remains that alcohol is the most commonly abused drug in our nation. Tobacco runs a close second. And each of these drugs is considered a "gateway drug" because they lead the kids who use them to try other, more dangerous drugs.

If we're going to talk to our kids about drugs, we need to first acknowledge that there actually *is* a drug problem. Then we need to consider the statistics about drug and alcohol use and abuse. Next, we can rejoice in the fact that the use of some drugs has actually gone *down* during the past decade. But there's an enemy in the drug wars that every parent and kid must be ready to face!

What Can Make the Drug and Alcohol Problem Worse?

What accounts for the steady worsening of the drug and alcohol problem? For one thing, take a look at the millions of dollars the liquor and tobacco industries spend bombarding us with television, magazine, and Internet ads encouraging us to drink—and drink often—to be "with it" and accepted. Kids watching those commercials want nothing more than to be accepted.

As far back as the 1980s, "The Bottom Line on Alcohol in Society" presented a summary of the strategy the liquor industry used to move kids from experimenters to habitual users of alcohol. In the decades since that report was first published, the industry's goals haven't seemed to change one bit:

- Increase the number of occasions on which current drinkers consume alcohol. The goal is to raise the number of times during the day when people drink, the number of days when they drink, and the number of occasions on which drinking is the thing to do.

- Increase the percentage of those who drink. In other words, turn the 90 percent of high school students who have experimented with alcohol into more regular users, especially when they reach the legal drinking age.

- Position alcoholic beverages to compete with soft drinks as "thirst quenchers" and "refreshment beverages." Evidence of this strategy includes corporate sponsorship of events and activities geared more toward teens and young adults; development of "alco-pop" products like wine coolers and malt beverages like "hard" lemonades and iced teas.[5]

Alcohol for Teens

The "alco-pop" phenomenon began during the 1980s with the introduction of "wine coolers," a mixture of wine and a carbonated, nonalcoholic drink often containing real fruit juice.

By 1991, the U.S. Department of Health and Human Services reported that 35 percent of all wine coolers sold in the United States were consumed by middle school, junior high, and senior high students.[6] And as their popularity increased, parents seemed to turn a blind eye and a deaf ear toward their influence.

A "Healthy" Addiction?

The wine cooler introduced kids and teens to alcohol that didn't taste like hard liquor. In addition, the fact that this product was basically disguised as something healthful made it easy to present as part of the lifestyle of those who have it "all together." Wine coolers were the "Kool-Aid" of kids in the 1980s. They hooked youngsters into the addiction process earlier, and because of children's fragile, developing bodies, locked them into that process more deeply and quickly than ever.

By the mid-1990s, however, the liquor industry took their aggressive campaign to lure younger and newer customers to the next level.

The Malt Beverage Revolution

Few if any teenagers really *like* the taste of hard liquor. But what if it's mixed with a fruit flavor like lemonade or prepared in such a way that it tastes more like iced tea? Add the luster of the name of an established alcohol brand, mix in a strategic marketing push pinpointing the "cool" youth lifestyle, and you have the makings of a revolution!

Before 1995, the mention of a "malt beverage" usually meant a flavored beer, typically malt liquor. They typically contained an alcohol content slightly higher than beer, but less than hard liquors such as vodka or gin. But in the mid-90s, the liquor industry began to expand with the advent of a new line of malt beverages aimed squarely at teens and young adults.

Smirnoff Ice, Jack Daniel's Country Cocktails, and Mike's Hard Lemonade were among the early market leaders in this product segment. And this "revolution" also led to a shift in the way even more mainstream alcoholic products were marketed. Cultural icons and mascots have been employed in recent years to establish a brand connection with younger consumers. Their efforts have been paying off. For example, a 1996 study by the Center on Alcohol Advertising showed that the Budweiser frogs were as recognizable to kids as Bugs Bunny.[7]

Drug Dangers Outside the Mainstream

Alcohol and tobacco companies operate as for-profit businesses in the U.S. They market their products through mainstream channels and sell them through recognized distributors. The government taxes their profitability and enforces the laws governing their business practices. Talking to your kids about the dangers of using those substances is relatively straightforward.

But just outside the public eye is the ever increasing crack and other illegal drug use, which is a strong economic force that is difficult to counter. Every gang member, every high school dropout selling drugs, and every pusher on every street corner is part of an industry propelled by a network of drug cartels based mainly in Colombia. These are sophisticated, well-organized, violent, underworld syndicates that have vast experience in drug trafficking. Their goal is to expand their markets and increase their profits at all costs, and they have plenty of money to invest in developing their market. The statistics show these organizations are achieving their goals—at the cost of our families and our nation's future.

The Damage Done

A study of 700 teenagers over a period of eight years revealed that heavy drug use leads directly to many problems. Young drug users divorce more quickly, suffer from greater job instability, commit more serious crimes, and are generally more unhappy with their lives and relationships than others. A generation of kids who are set up to fail in their personal and professional lives is a problem parents—and everyone else—must recognize and face.

We must be the transitional generation. Our kids are beginning to recognize how serious the problem is; now we must act to help them solve it. This isn't just a faddish project or charity. It's a deeply needed movement that must be headed by caring parents. The problem isn't getting better, and we must not wait for someone else to solve it for us. We must act one person at a time to drug-proof our children!

Chapter 3

How Do Kids Become Addicts?

Snow skiing is one of my (Jim's) favorite sports. Although I'm not exactly ready for the Olympics, I love the challenge of a steep slope filled with intimidating moguls. (My wife thinks I'm crazy.) I will never forget the first time I skied virgin powder. A stormy Colorado night gifted me with new snow. The conditions the next morning were perfect, and I was the first person off the chairlift. I plunged down on the two-foot-thick, feathery winter blanket left by Mother Nature.

To this day, I have never experienced more surges of adrenaline than I did when I started down that mountain. I was euphoric, and by the time I reached the bottom, I was on an incredible natural high. Breathless and eager to conquer the mountain again, I hoped those feelings of ecstasy would last forever. I have unsuccessfully tried to duplicate the experience time and again, spending thousands of dollars on additional ski trips and just the right equipment.

An Unnatural High

In many ways, especially at the beginning, taking drugs is similar to skiing fresh powder for the first time. It is an enchanting, intoxicating exhilaration. The experience really does help you lose sight of your problems. Everybody talks about the high. Curiosity, fear, and anticipation blur together, fogging the real consequences. Others have tried drugs and say it is great. It looks like fun, so why not give it a try?

Kids involved in drugs are like skiers who return to the top of the mountain after a great ride down the slope. They have tried a new substance. They have enjoyed the experience, so they head right back to repeat it again and again. Sometimes they go too far. They drink or smoke too much and get sick, but they try again because it's still the best "feeling" they have ever had. "It's better than sex," they say. "It's better than church. It's better than movies." Once they are hooked, they will compromise their lifestyles, steal, lie, beg, drop out of school, and turn from their faith to get back to the mountaintop.

My (Steve's) skiing experience was not like Jim's. I once boarded a gondola with three other teenagers. When the door shut and we headed up the hill, they reached into their jackets and pulled out three paper bags and a can of aerosol spray. They sprayed the vapors into the bags and inhaled deeply. Asking if they knew how stupid they were did no good. They wanted a high that surpassed the natural thrills offered by the slopes.

Recreational Use or Addiction?

Experimentation with drugs and alcohol is common. The vast majority of young people will try something, sometime. But besides physical addiction, what hooks them? Unfortunately, illicit drugs have two basic qualities that are terribly appealing.

Drugs Make Kids Feel Good

First, drugs make people feel good. Young people are moving from childhood to adulthood. Their bodies, minds, friendships, and spiritual lives are changing so rapidly that they are often bored, confused, lonely, alienated, or just plain unhappy. For those who don't cope well with all the new pressures, the substances dull their pain. Sure, it's a false sense of relief, but nevertheless, they feel better and life can go on.

Our children have been raised in the most drug-oriented society in history. Anything from menstrual cramps to migraines, baldness to loneliness, can supposedly be cured by a magical pill. "No reason to struggle." "No reason to hurt." "Take this." "Drink this. It will make you feel better." And the little magic substance does make kids feel better—for a while.

One time as I (Steve) sat in a room full of adolescent addicts, I asked, "Why?" After we cut through the garbage, they agreed on the root problem 100 percent: pain. Kids are living in emotional pain, and they want relief. But instead of finding real relief, they became addicted.

Drugs Always Work

The second reason drugs are so appealing is that kids believe they work every time. To them, drugs and alcohol are dependable, and family and friends, unfortunately, often are not. If kids are worried about family struggles, grades, loss of a sweetheart, or whatever, they count on the drugs or alcohol to make the hurt go away, at least temporarily.

6 Key Factors Leading to Drug and Alcohol Abuse

To prevent our children from becoming statistics, we must clearly understand how kids get started misusing drugs and alcohol. Experts estimate that between 85 to 95 percent of teenagers will experiment with alcohol and other drugs. It is unrealistic to think teenagers can be sheltered. Sometimes we see parents who seem to do everything right, but their kids are still substance abusers. More often, mental health professionals agree, the route to heavy substance abuse is mapped by the complex interplay of several factors. Here are six major reasons kids abuse drugs and alcohol.[1]

Biological Predisposition

It is almost universally agreed upon that a chemical dependency may be related to a genetic predisposition. Certain kids get hooked much faster than "normal." These kids *must* be told that because of their family backgrounds, they simply don't have the freedom to experiment. In any drug and alcohol treatment center, usually 50 percent of the patients come from families where a parent is an alcoholic. If both parents are alcoholics, the risk is much higher.

We (Jim and Steve) both have opportunities to speak to thousands of young people each year, and we have found that when kids are presented with the biological risk factor, they are more willing to change than when presented with scare tactics. When teenagers watch movies about substance abuse, complete with gory accidents and horrible stories, they often dismiss them with, "That will never happen to me." When confronted with the fact that many experts believe some people are genetically prone to alcoholism, however, the kids take notice. They want to talk. They want to find out more. They want to tell their stories.

Peer Pressure

Perhaps the strongest motivator for a young person to use is the desire for acceptance by peers. As mentioned in chapter 2, if your children's friends are experimenting with drugs or alcohol, the odds are great that your kids are also experimenting. If you suspect your children have drug problems because of the actions of their friends, don't wait for it to get better. It usually won't. Remember, where there's smoke, there's fire.

Preteen Drinking Story

One of my (Jim's) graphic memories is of the first party I attended in junior high. I had been invited to the party at the home of the most popular girl in our school. My dream of acceptance into that group had become a reality. I was honored, I was nervous, and this was the crowd I badly wanted to be accepted into forever.

As the party progressed, I noticed that some of the kids kept going out to the front yard and then rushing to the back patio looking as if they had a special secret. Out of curiosity, I followed them the next time they went out. I found Andrew with a bottle of tequila, pouring drinks for everyone, and this time he included me. I didn't want to drink, but the desire to be accepted was definitely more powerful than the desire not to drink. So I did what a majority of kids do. I drank the whole cup in one gulp. It ruined my time at the party. I hated the taste. I went home and threw up!

Positive Peer Influence

We can't simply assume our children will say no because we told them to do so. We must help them understand the influence their friends have on them. We must help build up their self-esteem because kids who have a positive self-image have more resistance to peer pressure. And we must take the time to get acquainted with our children's friends.

After 12 years of moving every few years, we (Jim and Cathy) decided it was time to settle down and stay a while. We looked for a neighborhood that included lots of kids our children's ages and chose a house conducive to children coming over and playing in the yard. We selected the house because we wanted to have our home "open to our children's world." Frankly, we wanted to know our kids' friends. Instead of spending money on appearance (after four years we still didn't have curtains in the living room), we invested in swing sets. Sometimes we got tired of being "Grand Central Station," but we were confident we knew our daughters' friends.

One day a wonderful fifth-grade neighbor, Sarah, came over and asked if our daughter Christy could play. I told her Christy and the girls were at the store with their mother and that I was the only one home. She replied, "Well, then, can you come out and play?" I put my work down and had a rousing game of soccer on our front lawn.

Parental Attitudes

The most important influence on children's attitudes about

alcohol and drugs is still the children's parents. Simply put, "Children see, children do." In many families, alcohol is a staple. Children never see their parents have a good time without alcohol. Many kids observe their parents drinking and driving regularly and get a double message: "You can't drink, but it's okay for me."

Despite dangerous consequences, it is common for parents to provide liquor for teenage parties. We've had parents tell us, "It's much better to allow our kids to drink at home and provide just beer for their parties. We always chaperone them."

You Are a Role Model

All studies show that the earlier children experiment with drinking and drugs, the more likely they are to become abusers because they learn to use chemicals to cope with natural development. If they feel anxiety, they use a drug to sedate that anxiety. Such kids stop learning how to handle stress. So one of the most important pieces of advice we can give parents is this: "Don't model alcohol or drug use. Period."

Ten years ago, when I (Steve) cautioned teenagers about the problems associated with drinking, they would commonly refer to their parents who drank. Today, they refer to parents who used drugs in the 1960s and 70s. These parents often don't care as much about their kids' use of drugs, and some continue to model the role of users.

Life Crisis

Like adults, children have to deal with stresses such as illness, divorce, or moving to a new community. As with adults, alcohol and drugs can serve to deaden the pain. I (Jim) recently had a woman tell me, "It wasn't until years later that I learned my son started drinking at 14½ when his father and I got a divorce." This woman was so absorbed with her own emotional and financial needs that it took a tragic accident to get her to see her son's problems.

Depression

Professionals who work with children and teenagers are observing a major increase in depression. The underlying causes of depression are complex, and we won't attempt to give a full psychological explanation. We do need to mention, however, that an angry or depressed child is prone to drug abuse.

A certain amount of depression is normal among teenagers. After all, the teen years are a time of rapid transitions. But certain warning signals can alert us to a problem, and if any of the following signals persist, we recommend you seek professional help for your child. The following signs are taken from the work of Dr. Ross Campbell.[2]

Warning Signs

If your child is only mildly depressed, you will notice an inability to keep his or her mind focused on a subject as long as usual. The attention span is shorter; the mind will drift, and your child will become easily distracted. A short attention span may be the first sign of depression.

Depressed or Just Bored?

Boredom is normal for teens, especially in early adolescence, but only for short time periods. When children are bored over a long period of time, they will look for stimulation. Research indicates that children who have low levels of imagination and lack creativity are more readily bored, and these children are more likely to turn to drugs. This is why it is important to encourage children, from a young age, to participate in athletics, drama, dance, music, art, or any other kind of creative activity. If you can keep your children from a crisis of boredom, you can help prevent problems in the future.

Somatic depression is a physiological depression that occurs when young people suffer headaches, stomachaches, or lower chest pains. The additional stress young people are experiencing today causes somatic depression to be common, and many turn to drugs or alcohol to medicate their pain.

Withdrawal from friends is another warning signal. Dr. Campbell explains it this way:

She will not just simply stay away from them [friends]. She will become belligerent...toward them so that the ensuing unpleasantness will result in total alienation.... Your teen will become very lonely and could very well start associating with unwholesome peers. This is where...peer influence comes in and can be the cause of initial drug experimentation. But as you can see...depression would also be the cause.[3]

Additional Symptoms

Dr. John Baucom has prepared another list of symptoms of depression to help you determine whether your child is depressed, and if so, how severe the depression is.[4] If you see your child clearly in this list, and the symptoms persist for an extended time, seek professional help.

Early Stages
>   Inability to concentrate
>   Excessive daydreaming
>   Withdrawal from friends
>   Impulsive acts, seemingly without forethought
>   Declining grades
>   Change in eating or sleeping habits

Middle Stages
>   Acts of aggression
>   Rapid mood swings
>   Loss of interest in work, school, etc.
>   Loss of friends
>   Boredom
>   Preoccupation with physical complaints
>   Mild rebelliousness
>   Sudden changes in personality

Danger Stage
   Visible depression
   Anorexia
   Alcohol or drug abuse
   Suicide threats, attempts, or gestures
   Giving away prized possessions
   Preoccupation with death
   Expressions of helplessness
   Loss of values
   Extreme aggressive behavior
   Overt rebelliousness

During a discussion of depression with kids in an adolescent treatment unit in Orange, California, a common thread was the shattering reality that life isn't easy. The kids "hit the wall" when they discovered life doesn't magically work out the way they wanted it to. Many of these kids were affluent; everything they needed had been given to them. It was too devastating for them to face their problems, let alone attack them. In the face of discomfort, they folded up into the emotional cocoon of depression. For many, drugs seemed the only way out.

Parenting Style

Too many parents are intent on being "buddies" with their children and do not take the responsibility of parenting seriously enough. Mental health professionals are unanimous: Children aren't getting enough supervision. Far too many parents have given up on investing the quality and quantity of time it takes to create a loving, firm, and caring environment.

A Case Study

A mother called me (Jim) to talk about her daughter's behavior. The girl was sneaking out of the house and getting drunk. The previous weekend the parents had changed their minds about staying overnight at a convention and had come home instead. This concerned mother described the party they had walked in on as "a full-blown, drunken orgy."

I welcomed the family to visit with me but I needed to see the mom, dad, and daughter together at the first appointment. I noticed the three of them arrived in three separate, expensive cars. As they began to talk, the parents mentioned they had an expensive house overlooking the Pacific Ocean. They also said both of them worked. Dad left the house at 6:15 in the morning and returned after 8:00 at night. They were experiencing intense financial pressure.

As the story unfolded, it became clear that both parents were working hard to pay for their beautiful house, the leases on three cars, and to put away money for their daughter's college fund. In the meantime, no one was taking any significant time to parent their needy daughter.

A Lifestyle Change for the Better?

I suggested meekly, "Have you ever considered moving to a smaller house, trading in your expensive cars, and working fewer hours to make your home something besides a place to sleep and fight?" They seemed to need permission to cut back on their fancy lifestyle and become a family again.

Months later the family called me. They had moved and traded in the nice cars. Mom was working only part-time, Dad came home for dinner, and their daughter had quit her "old life." She was looking forward to going to college after taking a few summer school classes to make up some of the time she had lost to the party scene. I wish all true stories could have such a happy ending!

Dignity, Respect, Love

Dr. H. Stephen Glenn, former director of the National Drug Abuse Center in Washington, D.C., says parents may be overly strict or overly permissive because they honestly believe this is the most loving thing they can do for their children. Their kids, however, may not perceive the loving part. "Children base their behavior on their perception of what is true, not on what is actually true," Glenn says. "Children are more likely to perceive loving intentions when tone of voice and actions convey dignity and respect along with firmness."[5]

Kids use drugs for many reasons. Hopelessness, rebellion, and the desire to feel like an adult are other reasons we often hear for taking drugs. We cannot afford to believe "it will never happen to our family."

The Path to Drug Abuse

When Terry's parents called to say they wanted to see me (Jim), I tried to talk them out of coming. After all, it sounded like a clear case of drug abuse in Terry's life. They needed a drug treatment program, not me. But they persevered. The day I met the family, I was shocked by their appearance and story.

They drove to my office in their beautiful new Mercedes. Instead of Terry looking like the street person I expected (from the stories his mother had told me), he was a clean-cut young man who was the star pitcher on his Christian high school baseball team. His parents were immaculate, articulate, and extremely concerned about Terry. Both were active in the church, and Terry had been raised in what truly appeared to be a model Christian home. My immediate reaction, although I knew better, was to dismiss Terry's drug problem as teenage experimental use, wish this family well, and move on to more pressing matters.

The Seeds of Addiction

When I was alone with Terry, I finally heard his story. At age 13 he went to a church camp. Some of the boys had sneaked in beer and wine. They were a little older than Terry, but because he was intelligent and a great athlete, they accepted him into the group.

The second night of camp, Terry drank the first beer ever offered to him. He wasn't sure about the taste, but he liked the acceptance of these older guys. Before the week was over, Terry had experimented with beer, wine coolers, and marijuana. He liked the high, and he liked the peer approval. He knew his parents would never approve. As a young Christian himself, he felt guilty, but he justified the experience, saying, "Even Jesus drank wine."

His experimental use turned to more regular use. He found a whole new world of kids who built their social lives around alcohol and marijuana.

A High Tolerance for Alcohol

Terry also noticed early in his drinking and drugging that he had an extremely high tolerance level. While other kids had three beers and either got so drunk they couldn't walk straight or they fell asleep or got sick, Terry could drink a six-pack and still be "in control."

A Dual Existence

Terry so enjoyed getting high that he began to think about it daily. "I was always figuring out when would be the next time I could drink or smoke marijuana." Some of his older friends introduced him to cocaine, saying it was the ultimate high. He tried it, loved it, and was hooked immediately. In his own words, "I became a slave to it."

At the same time, Terry was still trying to maintain his "Christian appearance." He was lying to his parents and found himself stealing alcohol from a neighborhood liquor store. Although he looked clean-cut and could still maintain the appearance of being straight most of the time, his grades, friendships, home life, and relationships with girls were beginning to slip.

The Progression of Addiction

Terry was one of the 3 million-plus teenagers who are chemically dependent. He had to get high to make it through the day, and he had a dangerous preoccupation with doing just that. His life had followed the typical stages of change in the list that follows.[6]

Frequently Seen Stages in Adolescent Chemical Use

1. Experimental Use
Late grade school or early junior high years

Intake

1. Occasional beer drinking, pot-smoking or use of inhalants (glue-sniffing, sniffing aerosols, etc.). Usually done weekends or during the summer, mostly with friends.
2. Easy to get high (low tolerance).
3. Thrill of acting grown-up and defying parents is part of the high.

What the World Sees

1. Often unplanned, using beer sneaked from home, model glue, etc.
2. Little use of "harder" drugs at this stage.

2. More Regular Use
Late junior high and early senior high years

Intake

4. Tolerance increases with increased use. More parties involving kegs, pot, possibly pills or hash. Acceptance of the idea that "everyone does it" and wanting to be in on it. Disdain of "local pot" or 3.2 beer. Staying out later, even all night.
5. Use of wine or liquor may increase, but beer remains the most popular drink. Willing to suffer hangovers.
6. Lying to parents about the extent of use and use of money for drugs.
7. Use on weeknights begins, and skipping school may increase.
8. Blackouts may begin, and talk with friends about "What did I do last night?" occurs.
9. Solitary use begins—even smoking at home (risk-taking increases). Concentration on fooling parents or teachers when high.

10. Preoccupation with use begins. The next high is carefully planned and anticipated. Source of supply is a matter of worry.

11. Use during the day starts. Smoking before school to "make it through the morning." Use of "dust" may increase, or experiments with acid, speed, or barbs may continue.

What the World Sees

3. More money involved, false IDs used. Alcohol or pot bought and shared with friends.

4. Parents become aware of use. May start a long series of "groundings" for late hours.

5. Drug-using friends often not introduced to parents.

6. Lying to parents about the extent of use and use of money for drugs.

7. School activities are dropped, especially sports. Grades will drop. Truancy increases.

8. Non-drug-using friends are dropped. Weekend-long parties may start.

3. Daily Preoccupation

Intake

12. Use of harder drugs increases (speed, acid, barbs, dust).

13. Number of times high during the week increases. Amount of money spent for drugs increases (concealing savings withdrawals from parents).

14. "Social use" decreases—getting loaded rather than just high. Being high becomes normal.

15. Buying more and using more—all activities seem to include drug use or alcohol.

16. Possible theft to get money to ensure a supply. May have a contact with "bigger" dealers.

17. Solitary use increases. User will isolate self from other using friends.

18. Lying about or hiding the drug supply. Stash of narcotics may be concealed from friends.

What the World Sees

9. Possible dealing or fronting for others.

10. Possible court trouble for minor consumption or possession. May be arrested for driving while intoxicated. Probation may result.

11. May try to cut down or quit to convince self that no problem with drugs exists.

12. Most straight friends are dropped.

13. Money owed for drugs may increase. More truancy and fights with parents about drug use.

4. Dependency

Intake

19. Getting high during school or at work. Difficult to face the day without drugs. Drugs are used to escape self.

20. Possible use of injectable drugs. Friends are burnouts (and may take pride in the label).

21. Can't tell what normal behavior is anymore—normal means being stoned nearly constantly.

22. Physical condition worsens. Loss of weight, more frequent illnesses, memory suffers, flashbacks may increase. Thoughts of suicide may increase.

What the World Sees

14. Guilt feelings increase. Questioning own use but unable to control the urge.

15. Low self-image and has self-hate. Casual sexual involvement. Continued denial of problem.

16. School dropped. Dealing may increase, along with police involvement. Parents may "give up."

17. Paranoia increases. Cost of habit increases with most of money going for habit.

18. Loss of control over use.

Thankfully, Terry's family has now seen him go successfully through a treatment center. They suffered an incredible amount of emotional stress and pressure in their marriage, not to mention spending tens of thousands of dollars to help Terry.

A Success Story

Tom and Linda Miramar are terrific parents. If you asked them, of course, they could tell as many "war stories" as the next family. Five years ago, however, they decided to learn all they could about drug and alcohol abuse. They were typical Christian parents who had a desire to keep their three children from experiencing the same pain as their older, alcoholic nephew.

When the Miramars' two boys and one girl were 10, 12, and 14, Tom and Linda came to me (Jim) and asked for every resource on drug and alcohol abuse I could offer. I gave them books, pamphlets, and tapes, and pointed out a few excellent (and free) educational seminars at a local treatment center. They put together a plan of education and prevention. They spent time discussing with their children what they had learned. The family made a contract that at the first sign of a problem, agreed-upon-by-all consequences would be put into action. To be a good role model, Tom also gave up his occasional cigar.

Last Christmas, I received a note from the family. It read: "Dear Jim: Concerning our Drug-Proof Plan, after five years, so far, so good. It was worth the investment. Thanks. The Miramar Family."

THE STATISTICS

Chapter 4

Cigarettes and Alcohol:
The Gateway to Drug Addiction

During my (Jim's) **early youth ministry days,** my wife, Cathy, and I were shopping at a local discount retail store. I'm a sucker for their "blue-light specials," and that day I found myself purchasing a pair of paisley, multicolored suspenders. They were ugly, but they cost me only $8.49 instead of $8.79. Such a deal! I had never worn suspenders, so Cathy had to show me how to put them on.

I proudly displayed my new purchase at our church youth group meeting the next evening. Because suspenders were not in style, the kids were intrigued by their youth pastor, to say the least. The next week, five students came to our group wearing suspenders. The following week, I was joined by nine others who had made the suspender purchase. (And they paid the full 30 cents extra!)

To be honest, I never wore the suspenders again—largely because the kids kept coming up behind me and snapping them against my back. But the fact that so many kids in the youth group followed my example and also bought the same type of suspenders reminded me again of the power of modeling. It is still the most influential educator. And if you want to talk to your kids about drug and alcohol abuse, your actions will *always* speak louder to your children than your words ever will.

Following Your Example

When faced with a new situation, oftentimes your kids will look to you to see how *you* handle it before they decide how they themselves will respond. It's only natural for a child to imitate his or her parents.

My (Jim's) oldest daughter is a study in contrasts in this regard. When she's having a conversation on the phone, she looks, acts, and sounds *exactly* like her mother. It's actually quite fun to watch— especially when the conversation gets interesting! At the same time, however, when she's angry, frustrated, or just plain pouty, she looks an awfully lot like her father…in fact, sometimes I get the feeling she's actually trying to imitate me, much to my dismay.

Like it or not, your children are copying your example. That being the case, we have to evaluate what behaviors we are modeling when it comes to how we handle alcohol and cigarettes.

One of the most powerful examples of modeling was presented a few years back in a commercial by the National Cancer Society. A father was shown smoking, followed by a little boy of about two mimicking everything Dad did. He found his father's cigarette package, pulled out a cigarette, and pretended to light up. The commercial finished with the caption, "Like father, like son."

Cigarettes Are "Gateway Drugs"

Kids who abuse drugs usually get started through "gateway drugs," as in Terry's case from chapter 3. Two studies found a constant progression of drug use among high school students. The pattern consistently followed four well-defined steps:

- Beer or wine
- Hard liquor and/or cigarettes
- Marijuana
- Other illicit drugs

Researchers report that virtually no one moves to step four without first going through steps one, two, and three. A sampling of New York college students supports this research. In this study, 99 percent of people who used illegal drugs regularly had started with tobacco and then moved on to marijuana.[1]

Based on the fact that alcohol and tobacco products are the easiest for teens and preteens to access, we'll spend the balance of this chapter focusing on these products' roles as "gateway drugs."

It Starts with a Cigarette

The National Institute on Drug Abuse reports that 13 percent of all teenagers currently use tobacco (compared to 29 percent of the total population).[2] Of all high school students, 22 percent are cigarette smokers. It's not surprising that so many kids are being enticed to start smoking; the cigarette industry spends just over $15 billion each year on advertising and promotional expenses related to their products. That works out to around $41 million *every day*.[3] As a result, the majority of adult smokers report that they started smoking by the age of 18. And every day, an estimated 3,900 young people under the age of 18 try their first cigarette.[4]

Eighty-five percent of those who experiment with cigarettes will become addicted to nicotine, some after smoking as few as five to ten cigarettes. Of these kids, 81 percent will try marijuana, whereas only 21 percent of nonsmokers will try it. Here is one instance where cold, hard facts speak volumes.

- Kids who smoke heavily are about 30 times more likely than nonsmokers to try illegal drugs.
- Pack-a-day smokers are:
    —45 times more likely than nonsmokers to have used marijuana in the past year

    —10 times more likely to use inhalants

    —79 times more likely to use cocaine[5]

In 1988, it was estimated that smoking killed more than 52,000 Americans each year through chronic lung disease. By 2006, that number had nearly doubled (90,600). Another 123,800 smokers died of lung cancer that year.[6]

All told, the National Institute on Drug Abuse estimates that approximately 438,000 deaths each year are now attributable to

cigarette smoking, resulting in direct medical costs of $75 bil-
lion.[7]

Legal but Not Logical

Just because tobacco is legal to smoke doesn't mean it is an intelligent choice. We like what some are teaching kids in kindergarten:
"Be smart, don't start." We often recommend that if children start
smoking, it will be considered irresponsible behavior worthy of a
parent's immediate attention.

Because cigarette smoking can lead young people into the world
of drugs, should parents smoke cigarettes? That depends on how
committed they are to raising drug-free children.

Why Kids Like Tobacco

Tobacco is a status symbol of rebellion, an external attempt at
maturity. Kids who have friends who smoke do it to feel accepted.
They have little adult interference; most parents who allow their
children to smoke do so because they themselves smoke. They don't
realize that if children smoke, they are probably using harder drugs
as well, especially marijuana. Nicotine produces a stimulating effect
until a person is addicted. Once the addiction is set, the person
becomes agitated if forced to go too long without nicotine. At that
point, the nicotine becomes a relaxing chemical that reduces the
agitation as it eases the withdrawal process.

How Tobacco Hurts Kids

Tobacco releases many carcinogenic chemicals into the bloodstream, brain, and central nervous system. Blood pressure is
increased, and the heart rate is increased up to 40 percent. Prolonged use may lead to lung and other kinds of cancer; mouth and
jaw cancer have killed many teenagers who use chewing tobacco.
The first step of rebellion against parents is often tobacco. Nicotine
is rarely the only drug a child uses.

Now, the chances are that if your child is in the "thinking about" stages of tobacco use, you're probably not going to find a carton of cigarettes in his or her bedroom. They'll want to keep their tobacco use a secret from you as long as possible. That's why it's important to make sure you "know the lingo" regarding the various names and forms of tobacco, and how it's most commonly used by kids.

What kids call it: Cigarettes, chew, puff, cigar, smoke, snuff.

Forms kids use: Cigarettes, cigars, snuff tins, and chewing tobacco in pouches.

How kids use it: Smoke or chew it.

Sara's Story

As a baby, Sara developed leukemia. She underwent chemotherapy until she was two, and since that time, she's been cancer-free. But that doesn't mean she wasn't tempted to try cigarettes.

When she started high school, Sara began to smoke. Soon she had a pack-a-day habit that lasted for nearly a year. Sara figured that since she had already defeated cancer as a little girl, she could beat it again if her smoking brought it back. Fortunately, it didn't—but Sara still had to come to her senses about how she was putting herself at risk by smoking. She's now 18 years old and has been cigarette-free for 3 years.[8]

The Gateway to Alcoholism

Alcohol is a dangerous drug even though our society mistakenly views it as separate from other drugs. Some parents are actually relieved to discover their kids are "only" drinking and not smoking pot or swallowing pills. But alcohol is a drug and a depressant, and it causes more deaths among young people than any other drug. Because it is legal and accepted by the general population, many people are unaware that it attacks the nervous system, and over a period of time, can shorten life.

In previous chapters, we've looked at some key statistics regarding the effects alcohol abuse can have on an individual and a family. In this next section, we'll consider the impact of alcoholism in society as a whole.

To begin with, the need for preventing alcohol and other drug problems is clear when examining the statistics:

- Nearly 5,000 young people under the age of 21 die each year from underage drinking.

- In 2006, nearly 1,900 deaths involving people under the age of 21 were the result of alcohol-induced automobile collisions (up from 1,400 in 1999).[9]

- 21 percent of the murders committed by young people were caused by alcohol.

- It is estimated that nearly 1 million nonfatal injuries each year are caused by underage drunk drivers. There are also approximately 1 million assaults committed by youth under the influence of alcohol; 40,000 cases of alcohol poisoning; and 5,100 injuries related to drunken suicide attempts by those under 21.[10]

What do you say to your kids about drugs through your example? Do you present an underlying message that you think they are not so bad? Are your children seeing your attitude as one of indifference? What drugs do you take? Reaching for a Valium or misusing sleeping pills are all part of a drug-taking picture a child forms, and you are the central actor. Are you willing to give up such things so your child can be free of drug and alcohol problems?

Troubled kids almost always point out the problems of excess in their parents. They say things such as, "My father doesn't drink, but you should see how much he eats. He's no better than I am. I use drugs, and he uses food." "My mother doesn't drink, but every time there's a crisis, she has to take some kind of pill. Why should she get on me if she has to have her own drugs?"

Whether it is excessive food, medication, or burying ourselves in our work, we parents must examine our compulsive behaviors. Our kids use them as part of a denial system that prevents change. But even more important, they model our bad behaviors.

The Best Alcohol Education

Kids are confronted with alcohol every day. It is a common topic of conversation at school and routine behavior for many kids in junior high and high school. So naturally, your children are going to be interested in *your* drinking behavior. They will watch you for clues that drinking is okay.

If you have been making mistakes in this area, it is not too late to stop and let your children see what it is like to start over. No lesson is more powerful than the example of an adult changing for the better.

The Power of a Positive Example

Many years ago Peter Marshall, former chaplain to the United States Senate, preached a sermon that had a profound influence on my (Jim's) life. In his sermon, he told a story that helped me make a decision to abstain from all alcohol.

He told of a minister who was asked to make a patriotic address at a dinner attended by many prominent government and business officials. It was a swank affair, and cocktails were flowing freely. Mr. Jones, who sat immediately to the minister's left, was greatly enjoying the alcohol. When Mr. Jones noticed the minister had an untouched glass of champagne in front of him, Mr. Jones stated, "Say, you haven't touched yours. Why not? Guess I'm rude to mention it, but surely you haven't any scruples against champagne?"

The minister replied, "No, you're not rude to ask at all." He went on to say, "I have a steady stream of people coming to my study who need help. Their lives are all messed up, and I guess you'd be surprised to know that most of them, in one way or another, have liquor involved in the mess. To drink this glass of champagne is no sin. However, because of so many who cannot control their alcohol use, I choose to be self-disciplined. I would never want anyone to justify his alcohol abuse by saying, 'Well, the minister drinks.' So I've chosen to abstain. It's not a matter of sin, but rather of example."

What Needs to Be Taught

Proverbs 22:6 tells us to train children in the way they should go, and when they are older, they will not turn from it. Is it any wonder we have such a high rate of alcohol and drug abuse when parents and kids spend so little time on the subject of training children? *Children who have the best chance of not doing drugs or alcohol come from families that have taken the time to train them—and during the preteen and adolescent years, this is especially vital.* If you can get children through those years drug free, their lives are almost guaranteed to be free from chemical abuse. Those who neither smoke nor drink as teenagers are mostly immune to later drug abuse. But parents who refuse to take the time to educate their children have a good chance of spending time trying to treat serious problems later.

The education part of a good drug-proof plan involves more than just knowing and teaching the facts about alcohol and drugs. Those are important elements, but the teaching must have a broader base, including the following three areas.

Responsible Versus Irresponsible Behavior

When I (Steve) first started working with drug addicts and alcoholics, I was amazed at the level of immaturity I saw. Many of these people told stories of how they stopped maturing when they started using drugs. Others told me they never learned to make decisions based on receiving rewards for good decisions and being disciplined for bad decisions. Many never had a model of responsible behavior, and even more were without someone to guide them toward it. So my job was to do for them what no parent had done before. I taught them the art of making responsible decisions. Don't neglect this important task for your children.

For example, suppose my (Jim's) daughter comes to me and asks, "Daddy, may I go to the beach with the Foster family today?"

I must help her see the whole picture, so I say, "You would have a great time at the beach with the Fosters. They're some of our best friends, and you're welcome to go with them most of the time.

However, we're having your sister's birthday party at the same time. Which do you think is more important?"

My goal is to let her make the right decision on her own. However, I may well hear, "But Rebecca has all her friends coming to the party, and she really wouldn't care if I wasn't there."

In that case, I may have to put my foot down and say, "Today you are not allowed to go with the Fosters because I believe it's more important for our family to celebrate Rebecca's birthday together." Although I had to impose my will, I still introduced the concept of thinking and choosing logically, not just emotionally.

Social and Communication Skills

Many kids today use alcohol and tobacco as a means of connection and building community with each other. As a result, that places an even greater importance on the fact that parents must take the time to teach children, through instruction and by example, to socialize and communicate *without* chemical assistance. Kids need to be exposed to social situations from a young age and shown how to relate to others in a relaxed manner. The edge of awkwardness needs to be rubbed off by caring parents. A child will then have less need to find social success in a bottle or a pill.

Positive alternatives to drugs and alcohol also need to be implanted in kids' minds. Parents can help a child find and develop some skill or talent so the child feels competent. Sports and the arts are good possibilities. They build self-esteem and fill time that might otherwise be used to do drugs.

The Dangers of Losing Control

One of the first people I (Steve) worked with was a girl who drank and used drugs. She was raped in a vacant house. Pregnancy, AIDS, other sexually transmitted diseases, and automobile accidents are real consequences of losing control. Take time to explain the possible consequences of drug use to your children. If you don't, they will see only the glamor of losing control as portrayed in movies and television.

All these areas of education form the foundation for prevention efforts that follow. Without education, the prevention efforts will fail.

You don't need to be an expert to put together a workable drug-proof plan. You must, however, become familiar with the facts. In the remainder of this chapter, you will find the necessary information to help make you a credible source in any discussion about alcohol. The illicit drugs of choice are presented in the chapters that follow.

Alcohol and Alcohol Abuse

Six thousand years ago, people discovered that drinking alcohol made them feel pleasantly different. Not long after, they discovered just how bad alcohol can make a person feel and what effects drunkenness and alcoholism can have. The problem of alcoholism was recorded in the first set of written laws. In about 3700 BC, the first brewery was established by the Egyptians. Today, the most commonly used drug in America is alcohol, and it is the drug of choice among teenagers.

The Biological Makeup of a Drinker

The effects of this chemical depend to some extent on the expectation of the drinker. The same amount of alcohol gets one person energized to go out and party but puts another to sleep in front of a television set. The setting also has a lot to do with the effect alcohol has on the user. In addition, alcohol has some paradoxical properties that produce different effects at different times.

Chemically, alcohol has a depressing effect on the central nervous system. If enough is consumed, it will depress the functions of the system to the degree that it will no longer signal the lungs to breathe or the heart to beat. But alcohol can also produce stimulating effects. Because it has calories that are readily absorbed and utilized, a person who has not eaten for a few hours takes a drink and obtains energy from it.

Alcohol is a food, a drug, and a poison. It is a food because it has calories. It is a drug because it alters moods. It is a poison because in large quantities it is toxic. Alcohol is also an irritating chemical. Pour it on a cut, and you immediately feel the irritation—pain. Imagine what effect that chemical has on sensitive nerve cells throughout the body!

Alcohol Tolerance

Many myths surround the use and abuse of alcohol. But the most destructive of all is the belief that being able to drink a large quantity of alcohol is a sign of strength. In reality, a high tolerance for alcohol—being able to "hold your liquor"—is a sign of budding alcoholism. It is the one thing all alcoholics have in common.

One day, we sat in an office with a teen and his parents listening to the teen's alcohol abuse story. He boasted he could drink a six-pack of beer without being fazed. In fact, he said he would drive others home after consuming 15 to 18 beers at a party. He was trying to make the point that he could handle liquor. Until we explained the reality of high tolerance, he didn't realize that he perfectly described his need for help to cure his disease of alcoholism.

How Well Do You "Hold Your Liquor"?

Most people have an automatic limiting mechanism that prevents them from developing a high tolerance to alcohol. Drunkenness, illness, or sleep occur when large quantities of alcohol are consumed. The tolerance level stays basically the same throughout life, though many would argue that a growing tolerance is developed over time. It is true that tolerance goes up a bit for most people, but for the alcoholic, the rise is either dramatic or tolerance is high from the first drink. In the world of drinking, the alcoholic veers off on a path that has only one end—addiction to the chemical.

Problem Drinking and Drunkenness

Alcoholism is not to be confused with *drunkenness.* Many alcoholics have such a high tolerance that they are rarely drunk. They drink a great deal but are often able to stop just before losing control. A family might live with an alcoholic for a lifetime and never see the person drunk. Only in the later stages of life, when a deteriorating and aging body loses its ability to contain vast quantities of alcohol, do many alcoholics drink until they lose control.

Drunkenness, however, can happen to anyone who has any level of tolerance. Some people are drunk on one drink. If that is the case, the Bible forbids them to drink because it condemns drunkenness, and rightfully so. Drunkenness is a big killer in our society.

The Bible clearly states, "Do not get drunk on wine, which leads to debauchery. Instead, be filled with the Spirit" (Ephesians 5:18). Drunkenness is a counterfeit for being filled with the Spirit. It is a form of escape and a maladaptive coping mechanism. Anyone who gets drunk is a problem drinker and needs help. The sin needs to be confessed, and the behavior changed. Unfortunately, when teenagers drink, most drink to get drunk. That is why teenage drinking is always considered problem drinking. It is illegal, and most of the time it is also immoral.

Alcoholism

Having been raised in Texas in a conservative Christian home, I (Steve) heard many sermons on alcoholism. The preacher always referred to the alcoholic as a drunkard. A biblical passage on drunkenness would be used to condemn that person, implying that the person had chosen alcoholism and would spend the remainder of his (they were always considered males) days in a drunken stupor.

Receiving this perspective early in life, my acceptance of the facts about alcoholism and drunkenness did not come easily. But eventually I learned the truth about the biblical perspective. It's been a great help in understanding alcoholics and assisting them in their recovery.

The Bible doesn't address the condition of alcoholism. It only speaks to us about drinking and drunkenness. Many ministers think of a drunk man on skid row drinking out of a bottle when they think of an alcoholic. But that is the *exception* rather than the rule. Only about 5 percent of all alcoholics make it to skid row. The other 95 percent are drinking and functioning in jobs, schools, churches, and in families. Many people have no idea these people are alcoholics.

The Alcoholic

An alcoholic is any person who consumes so much alcohol that he or she becomes addicted to the chemical. That is what alcoholism is—addiction to alcohol. If we understand that point, alcoholism is no longer a mystery. But the addiction is selective. Not everyone develops it. The reason is tolerance. People cannot drink enough alcohol to become addicted if they don't have a high tolerance for it. Anyone can abuse the chemical by getting drunk, but not everyone has the capacity to become an alcoholic.

These facts are the reason we have done so little to prevent alcoholism. One approach we use is to tell our children not to drink. But because 95 percent are going to try it anyway, we have to tell them *why* they shouldn't drink. Some tell teenagers not to drink because drinking is against the law. But they see adults break the law all the time, so the law is little or no deterrent. Some tell kids not to drink because drunkenness is condemned in Scripture. That can be helpful, but it does little to help the young person who is unknowingly sinking into addiction. There is a way, however, to communicate in a rational manner that helps kids understand the reasons to abstain from alcohol.

Scaring Kids Away from Alcohol

In the past, whenever I (Jim) would speak on drugs and alcohol at youth events, such as high school assemblies or youth conferences, I would tell stories that would try to scare kids out of drinking. I'd talk about the skid row stories of drug overdoses. My implication was that chances were good this could happen to them. I am not convinced, however, that this method worked very well. Sure, the kids would listen to the stories, but I believe most of them walked away saying, "That will *never* happen to *me*."

A More Authentic Approach

Now I share a much more rational message. It basically focuses on our bodies' predisposition to alcoholism. If we come from a family that has a history of alcoholism, we have a much greater chance of becoming alcoholics. I remind the kids that alcoholics have a very high tolerance for alcohol. In other words, alcoholics can consume vast amounts of alcohol and not actually be drunk, as long as they drink below their tolerance level.

One student came to me and said, "My dad's an alcoholic, and you're telling me that I have a greater predisposition to be an alcoholic because it could be hereditary?"

I said, "Yes."

He said, "That's not fair."

I said, "Life's not always fair."

He said, "You may not believe this, but I can drink six beers at a party and not get drunk."

I said, "I believe it. In fact, you may be less drunk with six beers in you than someone who drank two beers." I went on to say, "You are a budding alcoholic."

He said, "I don't even get drunk very often."

I replied, "That's because you drink below your tolerance level, which, as with all alcoholics, is high."

What I was trying to get across to this student was that many alcoholic teenagers can consume vast amounts of alcohol and, because their bodies have high tolerances for alcohol, they will not be as drunk as the kid who drinks two wine coolers and falls asleep or is dizzy drunk. Many of the high-tolerance alcoholics are praised by their peers for their ability to hold liquor, but in reality they are alcoholics. As they get older, their bodies will break down and accept alcohol differently. They will tend to get drunk quicker. The rational approach works.

The Sin Issue

Some of you reading this are no doubt eager to know whether we believe drinking is a sin. This is a difficult area; Christians hold varied views. However, from our study of Scripture, our work with thousands of young people, and our own experiences, we have arrived at the following beliefs. We don't expect everyone to agree, but we hope this list will stimulate the reader to think through his or her stance.

Drunkenness is always a sin. Scripture is clear on this, a fact that can't be rationalized away. Those who repeatedly become intoxicated need to confess their sin and obtain whatever help is needed to overcome it. Parents should sit down with their children to explain the sinful nature of drunkenness and why God has so clearly forbidden it.

Drinking is definitely a sin for some people. For the general population, no specific Scriptures forbid wine consumption in small amounts. Some Scriptures do, however, forbid alcohol consumption if it causes another person a spiritual problem. Whenever a spouse is bothered by the other spouse's drinking, for instance, it is the drinker's responsibility to stop drinking to prevent the mate from stumbling. But the rightness and wrongness of drinking is an even broader issue.

In our society, with so much damage being done by drinking, many who think it is okay to drink need to reexamine the practice. Alcohol is a dangerous chemical. A person may not drive drunk, but we now know that alcohol damages brain cells and other body tissues. And for us parents who have to be concerned about the behaviors we are modeling, abstinence is the best choice.

Alcoholism is an issue separate from sin. This condition develops from years of (often abusive) drinking, so sin occurs long before the onset of alcoholism. When a person develops alcoholism, compassion rather than judgment should be offered. Direction instead of condemnation is needed. The alcoholic—addicted, sick, and irrational—will respond better to the love of a helpful person than to the anger of one who doesn't understand. Is alcoholism a sin? The more important question is whether you are prepared to help a fellow sinner.

The Alcoholism Progression

Most people think alcoholics are weak people who cannot cope with life. That is not true. In all my years of working with them, I (Steve) have rarely seen a weak alcoholic. What I usually see is a person of phenomenal strength and stamina. Only a strong person could go to work hungover, be in withdrawal, crave a drink, have nerves agitated and irritated, and still function well for years. Only in the latter stages do I find the effects of alcoholism producing weakness within the person.

The results of alcoholism are not the cause of alcoholism. This is best understood by tracing the progression of the problem through the four common steps.

Tolerance

Tolerance for alcohol rises to a level that allows the body's cells to adapt to the chemical. Alcoholics become addicted to the chemical and process it more easily than other substances. This forms the basis for craving the chemical. Eventually, alcoholics do not drink to feel better but to feel normal because the body becomes dependent upon the chemical. They function better having it in their system than without it. The normal person watches performance decrease as more alcohol is consumed. Alcoholics watch their performance improve as more alcohol is consumed, as long as the drinking stays below the level of tolerance.

Toxicity

The delicate chemical balance in the brain is disrupted when it is saturated with alcohol's toxic chemical. The liver is not able to remove all the toxins from the alcohol consumed, so the toxins collect in the brain and disrupt its natural functions. Thinking, feeling, judging, remembering, and choosing are all distorted because the brain is sick. Sick brains produce sick behavior.

Psychological and Spiritual Problems

Living with a sick brain results in a life full of personal problems. If you don't believe this, spend one day in the ward of a drug and alcohol treatment center or one evening at an Alcoholics Anonymous meeting. You will meet people on the road to recovery whose lives are strewn with damaged relationships. They may have become detached from their spouses and children. The ability to concentrate has faltered, and job performance has declined. Morals have also declined as judgment has been destroyed. And we can expect that these people will feel guilty and alienated from God.

Physical Deterioration

In the last stages of alcoholism, the body deteriorates. The liver breaks down, the stomach develops ulcers, the lungs stop working, and the irritation of the chemical often produces cancer. The body was not meant to be saturated with a toxic chemical, and over time it breaks down because of it.

Alcoholism is not the simple choice most people believe it to be. *Drinking* is a choice. *Drunkenness* is a choice. But alcoholism is more complicated, especially because of genetic predisposition, which was discussed earlier. I (Steve) was amazed to see how many alcoholics had alcoholic parents. Such a predisposition might grow out of seeing a parent as a practicing alcoholic, but I believe it goes deeper.

Suppose a mother drank while pregnant. The baby would also be drinking (secondhand) and could get drunk. If the mother nursed the child while drinking heavily, the baby would continue to consume alcohol and perhaps start the addiction process.

Some people are born with a high tolerance to alcohol. This ability to drink more than a normal amount could come from a father or a grandmother who had a high tolerance; such tolerance levels are a common thread in alcoholic families.

All these factors hint at a condition that goes beyond the choices of drinking and drunkenness. Alcoholism isn't just a repetition of bad decisions or irresponsibility.

The information presented here is what every alcoholic and budding alcoholic comes to understand. It is the body, not the mind, that becomes addicted to the chemical. That being the case, an alcoholic must stop drinking forever. He or she cannot become smart enough, good enough, or spiritual enough to drink safely. Mental, emotional, and spiritual growth does nothing to change an addicted body. And once the addiction process is started, it can never be stopped. (God can always heal the body, of course, but we are talking about the normal flow of events, not the miraculous.)

The Essential Facts

To summarize, the essential facts we need to communicate to our kids about alcohol, alcohol abuse, and alcoholism are:

- Alcohol is an addictive chemical used in many popular beverages, and as with any addictive drug, if you consume enough, you will become physically hooked.

- Relatively few people become addicted to alcohol (about 20 percent of the people who drink) because most do not have a high tolerance for the chemical. They get sick or drunk or fall asleep before reaching the addictive level.

- The key to becoming addicted is tolerance. In our society, tolerance is applauded as a sign of strength. Being able to "drink someone under the table" is a badge of honor. But the ability to hold your liquor is *not* a positive sign; it is negative, an indicator of developing alcoholism.

Those who have a high tolerance while young become adults who cannot stop drinking.

- Those who don't have a high tolerance for alcohol are subject to problem drinking and drunkenness. Drinking to get drunk is irresponsible behavior specifically condemned in the Bible. It *always* causes problems and is *always* a sin. Drunk driving is the leading killer of adolescents. Drunkenness is also a prelude to getting high on other drugs; alcohol is a gateway drug. One thrill is replaced with a more dangerous one. The key is not to start looking for the thrill.

- A person who needs to get drunk repeatedly needs help. He or she is in pain and is seeking relief in a bottle. Many other and better ways to manage emotional pain are available, ways that make the pain diminish, not grow. Drinking to kill the pain only increases the pain when the drinking stops. The greatest consequences of drinking to get drunk are death and lack of developing maturity. Consequences may also include pregnancy and other results of poor judgment caused by intoxication.

- People who have a high tolerance for alcohol need to stop drinking. If it is early in their drinking, they need to make the decision to stop before they become addicted and cannot stop. If they are already past the point of being able to make a rational decision, they need professional help.

In relaying this information, you aren't just telling children not to get drunk; you are pointing out why. In addition, you address the alcoholism problem in present terms of high tolerance rather than in terms of the future. Kids don't care what might happen in ten years. Help them see why drinking is a problem *today.* When they understand alcohol is addictive and high tolerance allows the addiction to develop, they may decide to stop drinking.[11]

Chapter 5

Marijuana and Prescription Narcotics: The Dangers for Teens

Imagine you're taking a relaxing drive with the one you love through the magnificent Northeast. It's autumn, so the leaves have just begun to change. You've never seen anything quite that beautiful—and so, sensitive and romantic soul that you are, you decide to pull to the side of the road and gather up a few of the fallen leaves as momentos of your visit.

You wind up picking a couple of garbage bags full of the leaves and proceed to stuff them in the trunk of your car. Once the job is done, you drive to a gas station just down the road to fill up your tank and use the restroom. After you wash up, you're back on the road again.

About 30 minutes later, you begin to have some strange sensations—your face feels flushed, and you become lightheaded. Something is happening that you don't quite understand. And then the discomfort of a lifetime flares up. You can't sit still. You itch and itch and itch as you have never itched before. Nothing you do seems to help. The itching grows worse and worse the longer you drive.

By now you've figured out the cause of this uncomfortable and embarrassing problem. While picking up some beautiful leaves, you inadvertently got into poison ivy and spread the oil of that plant to places on your body you wished you hadn't. It'll take weeks for the symptoms to finally subside, but you've learned a valuable if not painful lesson—all is not as it appears on the surface. Some of the most beautiful and appealing things produce the worst consequences.

The Lure of Illicit Drugs

We must help our children understand that lesson because television, movies, and advertising show us a side of alcohol and illicit drugs that is very appealing. What you see is glamor, belonging, being cool, freedom, and great times with great feelings.

Advertisers can't sell alcohol by showing bums on skid row drinking out of a bottle. They don't show pictures of kids whose heads were cut off while going through the windshield of a car driven by a drunk or spaced-out driver. Drug dealers never show kids the prostitute who used to be an honor student but now turns tricks to support her cocaine habit. Drug pushers offer the first couple of "hits" free because they know that once a kid is hooked, he or she will pay just about any price to keep trying to top that initial high.

Kids must be taught that appearance is not always reality—especially when it comes to illicit drug use and abuse. That kind of authenticity is a key component if you want to successfully talk to your kids about drugs. And if those kids are in high school, their peers who use have probably moved beyond cigarettes and beer and on to the next two most influential gateway drugs—*marijuana* and *prescription narcotics*.[1]

Marijuana

Smoking marijuana usually becomes the springboard to heavier drug use. According to a recent edition of the National Drug Threat Assessment compiled by the U.S. Drug Enforcement Administration, 14 percent of all teenagers will use marijuana this year. Of all eighth graders, 12 percent will try it for the first time during the next 12 months, increasing to 26 percent of all tenth graders. And an astonishing 33 percent of all high school seniors (1 in 3!) will smoke a joint sometime during the next year. Of marijuana users, 67 percent progress to other drugs! However, 98 percent of those teens who *do not* smoke pot *do not* take other drugs.[2]

We attended junior and senior high school in the late 1960s. Timothy Leary and other drug heroes were saying marijuana was not harmful. They also said it was less dangerous than alcohol and caused no hangover. Our generation generally believed this to be true, and at the time no substantial studies proved the contrary.

All that has changed, however. For one thing, today's marijuana is up to 20 times stronger than the plants harvested only a decade ago. Furthermore, it has been substantiated that not only does pot have more cancer-causing agents than tobacco, but it also destroys brain cells and harms short-term memory retention.

Continued use of marijuana can lead to what is called "amotivational syndrome"—lethargy, reduced attention span, varying degrees of personality change, and general lack of interest in anything but getting high. Marijuana also diminishes the body's ability to protect itself from illness by reducing the division of disease-repelling white blood cells. A person who smokes marijuana regularly is likely to get sick more often than is normal. Marijuana is not the harmless drug of the psychedelic '60s but a treacherous gateway to heavier drug use.

The following is a description of marijuana and its derivatives, along with a basic overview of the effects it can have on its users.

Cannabis (marijuana, hashish, and THC)

Why kids like it: The marijuana high is euphoric for most users. Its general effects are relaxation and calm. Most users claim it stimulates and enhances the senses.

How it hurts kids: The drug reduces short-term memory and hampers the ability to concentrate. Acute panic, anxiety, and an intense fear of losing control are common. The more than 400 chemicals in the smoke cause cancer, a risk that is increased because the smoke is deliberately held in the lungs longer than cigarette smoke. The drug causes a severe strain on the cardiovascular system, raising the heart rate as much as 50 percent. The mood-altering chemical THC affects hormones in men and causes a temporary loss of fertility. Male marijuana users experience a higher level of abnormal sperm.

One of the biggest problems with marijuana is that it is a gateway drug into other, more damaging chemicals. After prolonged use, a phenomenon called "amotivational syndrome" can set in. When this happens, the child loses motivation to achieve, and grades plummet, along with performance in other activities. Automobile accidents are common because reaction time while driving can be reduced by 40 percent.

What kids call it: Pot, grass, reefer, weed, herb, smoke, joint, dope, J, bud, bag, dime, quarter, hashish, hash, getting high, getting wasted, getting stoned, getting loaded, Mary Jane, sinsemilla, Acapulco Gold, Thai sticks, shake, bong load, hootch, doobie, sins.

Forms kids use: Loose leaves that look like dried parsley, black gunny bricks, oval-shaped seeds, black-to-clear liquid, and THC pills.

How kids use it: Smoking roll-your-own cigarettes called joints; smoking with a bong; eaten in cakes, brownies, or cookies; pipes (sometimes made out of pop cans); and taking soft, gelatin capsules for concentrated THC.

Prescription Narcotics

In generations past, most teens had little use for taking prescription narcotics to get high. But with the desire for a cheap "buzz" combined with easy access via the worldwide web, it's easy to see why prescription narcotics have become the second most common form of drug abuse (after "gateway drugs") among teenagers. Approximately 1 in 10 teenagers is abusing prescription narcotics at present.[3]

Prescription medications like pain relievers, tranquilizers, and stimulants *can* be very useful for treatment when taken as directed.

Pain relievers make surgery possible, and often enable those with chronic pain to live more manageable lives. However, when these medications are taken without the guidance of a qualified medical professional, addiction is often the result.

Here are some of the more common forms of prescription medications and how they are used and abused.

Sedative-Hypnotics (barbiturates, tranquilizers, methaqualone, depressants)

Why kids like it: Small amounts produce a relaxed state similar to drunkenness. The user feels a sense of well-being, and has few inhibitions.

How it hurts kids: Large doses can cause respiratory depression, coma, and death. Psychological dependency is easily developed, as well as addiction with its severe withdrawal symptoms of panic, anxiety, and even death from convulsions. This withdrawal can sometimes be more severe than heroin withdrawal. Driving under the influence kills kids because the drugs slow reflexes and impair judgment. Death from overdose often occurs when these chemicals are mixed with other drugs, such as alcohol.

What kids call it: Downers, barbs, blue devils, red devils, yellow jackets, yellows, Nembutal, Seconal, Amytal, Tuinals, Q's, ludes, rainbows, candy, tooies, doing downers, on downs, Doriden, Quaaludes, Valium, Librium, Equanil, Miltown, Serax, Tranxene, Zanax.

Forms kids use: Capsules in colors of white, yellow, red, blue, red-and-blue; liquid; powder; tablets; suppositories.

How kids use it: Pills and capsules are taken orally or crushed, dissolved, heated in liquid, and then injected.

Narcotics (heroin and prescription drugs)

Why kids like it: The initial euphoric high is accompanied by a feeling of relaxation and relief from anxiety.

How it hurts kids: Death can come from overdose, and addiction is almost guaranteed from repeated use. Death can also result from convulsions in an overdose or through the withdrawal process. AIDS, hepatitis, and other diseases are transmitted by dirty needles. The unpredictability of the strength of the drug can also lead to death from overdose, for example, Mexican brown heroin can be as much as 40 times stronger than the more common white powder.

What kids call it: Snow, H, smack, stuff, junk, Harry, boy, China white, c-and-w, balloon, dope, horse, white, brown, mud, gum, chiva, being wasted, being stoned, slamming, banging, shooting up, on the nod, nodding, cooking, black tar, tar, dolophine, methadone, amidone, codeine, pectoral syrup, pethidine, Mepergan, paregoric, Parepectolin, Dover's powder, Percocet, Percodan, Fentanyl, Darvon, Talwin, Lomotil, cheese.

Forms kids use: Capsules, tablets, white crystals, liquid, dark-brown sticky bars, powder.

How kids use it: Injected, smoked, or eaten.

We live in a culture where it might seem to kids like there's a remedy for every ailment. The reality is that there is *not.* Talk to your kids about the reasons why certain medications are only available with a prescription from a qualified and licensed medical doctor. An ongoing dialog with your kids about the dangers of prescription drug abuse can go a long way toward keeping your kids drug-free!

Chapter 6

Inhalants and Over-the-Counter Drugs: The Dangers for Preteens

The clock on the wall of her seventh grade Spanish class read 9:17. *That can't be right,* Amanda thought. *It feels like we've been in here for an* hour—*and it's only been* five *minutes?*

Her best friend, Kaitlyn, sat next to her in class. She gave Amanda her best "I am so *bored*" glance. Then, as she turned her attention back to the front of the room where their teacher was droning on with that day's dialog, she handed Amanda a note.

She tried not to look too conspicuous as she opened the half-folded paper and read it silently to herself. It said, "I think I'm getting a cough. ☺ "

Amanda smiled to herself. She turned to her best friend and caught her glance. The two exchanged a nod and a knowing smile. Then Amanda added to Kaitlyn's note, "44 party at my house after school?" and handed it back across the aisle.

Kaitlyn read the response, scribbled a large "K" on the outside flap, and placed it on Amanda's desk, just like she always did. It was part of the ritual these two young girls had developed over the school year. Once their day at school was done, they would collect their books and backpacks and walk the short distance to Amanda's house. There they'd get high on cough syrup.

Middle School Drug Abuse

It's fairly well-known that many teenagers struggle with substance abuse. But what's becoming more widespread is the number of pre-teenagers who are also developing chemical addiction. The reason for the surprise among many parents is the fact that these "tweens" (kids between the ages of 8 and 12) are using nonprescription drugs like cough syrup to get high.

The common ingredient is dextromethorphan, a safe and effective active ingredient in many nonprescription cough syrups, tablets, and gel caps. When taken according to the recommended dosage, it helps control and quiet coughs with little if any long-term damage to the user. But when taken in excessive amounts, it can produce a high that many middle-school-age kids want to experience.

Common side effects to dextromethorphan include confusion, dizziness, blurred vision, abdominal pain, and nausea. And if the cough medication includes other ingredients to treat multiple symptoms, those complications can increase. Other at-risk areas for kids include any over-the-counter (OTC) medications containing alcohol. Make it a point to read labels carefully before considering which OTC remedies to keep in your home.

Many middle schoolers are led to abuse cough syrup and other OTC (or nonprescription) medications because they're led to believe that these meds are safe. Don't believe it—and make sure your kids know the truth as well.[1]

Inhalants

An inhalant is any breathable chemical vapor that produces a mind-altering effect. Middle-school-age kids sometimes turn to "huffing" because it's a pretty easy high to get. Many household solvents and cleaning products, art supplies, office supplies, and common aerosol propellants all contain the chemical makeup to give a kid a mild to moderate buzz in fairly short order.

The use of inhalants hits its peak during the middle-school years. In one recent study, 17 percent of all eighth graders surveyed indicated they had used inhalants during the past year. That number dropped to 13 percent of all tenth graders and 11.4 percent of the high school seniors surveyed.[2]

There are more than 1,000 common products that can be used—or should we say *misused*—as inhalants. Here's a breakdown of the categories and how they can harm our kids.

Inhalants (solvents, glue, gases, nitrous oxide, amyl and butyl nitrite, hydrocarbons, chlorohydrocarbons)

Why kids like it: Inhalants are cheap and easy to obtain and use. They have a stimulating effect, along with euphoria. At higher doses, the user loses inhibitions and sometimes total control.

How it hurts kids: Initial negative effects of inhalants include nausea, sneezing, coughing, nosebleeds, fatigue, lack of coordination, and loss of appetite. Judgment is impaired, and heart and respiratory rates are decreased markedly. Kids commonly have a loss of self-control that can include violent behavior. Some kids become unconscious after inhaling, and some even die. Suffocation can occur when a high concentration of the chemical replaces oxygen in the body and depresses the central nervous system to the point that breathing stops. It is not uncommon for kids to choke on their own vomit while unconscious. Hepatitis and long-term brain damage are results of heavy use, along with permanent damage to the central nervous system that can produce anxiety attacks and paranoia for a lifetime. Central nervous system damage also decreases mental and physical functioning. Specific harm to bone marrow, kidneys, liver, and blood is possible.

What kids call it: Laughing gas, whippets, poppers, snappers, rush, bolt, locker room, bullet, climax, glue, aerosol, vapors, solvents, gunk, buzz bombs.

Forms kids use: Airplane glue, nail polish remover, lighter and cleaner fluid, gasoline, paint, hair spray, whipped cream cans, and other aerosol dispensers.

How kids use it: Sniffing directly from source, inhaling vapors directly, or using a paper bag to concentrate fumes and gases. They also use a small metal cylinder attached to a balloon or pipe.

"Wheels"—A Case Study of Inhalant Abuse

Margaret Wagner never thought of herself as an *angry* parent. She had no reason to be. She was the mother of three wonderful children and lived with her family in the scenic Northeast. The youngest of her three children was her son Keith, an active youngster who used to move so fast his classmates gave him the nickname "Wheels."

Keith was bright, popular, and a good athlete. He never gave his parents any reason to suspect there was anything wrong in his life. But one mysterious night in August of 1998, everything changed for the Wagner family.

Keith had planned to see a movie with a couple of friends, but their plans changed. Instead, they wound up hanging out at a local mall. With his 11:00 curfew fast approaching, Keith called his mother and asked for "a little more time" to hang out with his pals. His mom was too tired to argue with him that evening so she relented, and Keith's curfew was extended to midnight.

While they were out and about, a couple of Keith's friends had secured some aerosol cans and began huffing. High on the fumes, one of the friends got behind the wheel of the car. He passed out while driving. The car swerved out of control and crashed straight into a stone wall. The impact of the crash drove the vehicle past the barrier and into a nearby tree. The force of the crash was so strong that the vehicle's engine was knocked from its mounts and hit Keith in the chest. The paramedics who responded to the scene reported that Keith Wagner was DOA.

An Angry Mom

After her son's death, Margaret Wagner wanted answers. She wanted to know why her son died such a tragic death. She wondered how he and his friends could have become addicted to inhalants without their parents ever suspecting anything was wrong. She was amazed that the driver of the vehicle, who was responsible for her son's death, was only ordered to surrender his driver's license for two years and perform 250 hours of community service.

Margaret Wagner did not want her son to have died in vain. And he didn't.

Keith's Law

Margaret Wagner took her cause to the Internet and came to the attention of New Jersey State Senator Anthony Bucco. He asked her to testify before the State Safety Commission about amending the state's DUI law to include inhalant abuse. She did—and it was. Today the legislation known as Keith's Law makes the use of inhalants, vapors, and fumes a crime chargeable by *evidence* only when involved in a motor vehicle accident (i.e., a blood test proving intoxication is not required for conviction). Through her heartache and pain she has been able to bring about reform. But no matter how many lives Keith's Law might save, it will never bring back the one most important to Margaret Wagner.[3]

Other Stimulants

Amphetamines, Methamphetamines, and Ritalin

Why kids like it: These drugs produce a state of excitation and energize the user. They feel invincible. This allows the user to stay up or come out of a depression that might be caused by withdrawal from another drug. Some kids use the chemicals to study for long hours. Others use them as an appetite suppressant in controlling weight. The high from these stimulants can last up to two hours, giving the user a state of false confidence and pseudo-productivity.

How it hurts kids: Heavy use can cause death from stroke or heart failure. Tremors, loss of coordination, headaches, blurred vision, anxiety, skin disorders, ulcers, vitamin deficiencies, and malnutrition are results of chronic use. Excessive amounts can also cause an amphetamine psychosis with hallucinations, delusions, and paranoia, as well as permanent brain damage. Kids easily become addicted to the drugs because tolerance develops quickly. Users feel a sense of constant energy until the body can no longer tolerate the drug, and then the child has a complete physical collapse. The drugs on the street are often look-alike drugs that contain little or no amphetamine. This can cause a child to believe his or her tolerance is greater than it really is and leads to overdose when the kid happens to purchase the actual substance. Toxic chemicals passed off as amphetamines can also cause permanent brain damage.

What kids call it: Speed, white cross, white devils, uppers, dexies, bennies, LA turnabouts, black beauties, pep pills, bumble bees, copilots, hearts, Benzedrine, Dexedrine, footballs, Biphetamine, crank, lid poppers, wake ups, popping uppers, speeding, being wired, flying, crystal meth, crystal, crystal Methedrine, mother's little helpers, Preludin, Didrex, pre-state, Voranil, Tenuate, Tepanil, Pondimin, Sanorex, Plegine, Ionamin, fast.

Forms kids use: Capsules, pills, tablets, yellowish and white crystals, and waxy rocks that resemble blocks of paraffin.

How kids use it: Taken orally (sometimes they are mixed with cocaine, then rubbed on teeth, tongue, and gums); inhaled through the nose; injected directly into the bloodstream by crushing pills or tablets, dissolving them in liquid, and heating them before drawing them up into a syringe.

The middle school years are tough enough without your children having to deal with the revelation that drugs can be so easy to get and use. Start talking to your tweens about drugs and alcohol—and then keep it up as an ongoing dialog.

Chapter 7

Drugs at Your Doorstep: What You Need to Know About Crack and Cocaine, Ecstasy, Heroin, LSD, and PCP

If the drug problem were limited to three or four drugs...or even just a couple of *types* of drugs...it would be much easier on us parents to talk to our kids about drugs and help keep them drug-free. But the fact is, there are several different kinds of drugs in the culture today...and improperly using even one of them only once can prove deadly for our children.

Almost every day a new term is developed for a new chemical substance found on the street. Some of these terms stick, and some disappear quickly, but the drugs are always pushed as a ticket to happiness. Well, the reality is that this is a lie. For this reason, we're devoting the balance of this chapter to giving you the facts you need to know about the other major illicit drugs on the market. Then we'll take a look at some practical principles you can use to keep your kids drug-free.

We haven't tried to include every term or every bit of information being used in schools or on the street. That would be impossible. We have included the most heavily used substances and the most common names for them. This information won't make you hip or cool, but it will enable you to converse intelligently with your children about the substances being passed around. You will also be able to discuss the dangers of each chemical, along with why that particular drug is so widely used.

Cocaine and Crack

Why kids like it: It is cheap and readily available. The stimulating, euphoric effect hits quickly and lasts for 5 to 30 minutes.

How it hurts kids: Cocaine is the most addictive drug known to humankind. When its extreme euphoria wears off, it leaves the user depressed and often suicidal. Frequent violent behavior is manifested, and kids can hurt or kill each other in these outbursts. The mucous membrane of the nose can become ulcerated from chronic use. Injecting cocaine with unsterile needles transmits AIDS, hepatitis, and other diseases. The highly volatile gases used to freebase the drug sometimes explode, and the child burns to death or is severely scarred. Death can occur when the drug disrupts the brain's control of the heart and respiration. Cocaine also causes angina, heart palpitations, and arrhythmia.

What kids call it: Coke, rock, freebase, flake, blow, snow, crack, C, toot, base, dynamite, girl, snorting, doing a line, lady, baseball, crank, coffee, shoot, foil, sniffing foil, dandruff.

Forms kids use: White or yellowish powder or paste, beige or light-brown pellets, white crystalline rocks resembling coagulated soap. These are often distributed in small plastic bags or vials.

How kids use it: Inhaled (also includes placing it on tinfoil, heating the foil underneath with a lighter, and breathing in the fumes—this is called "foiling"); smoked; injected with intravenous needles; dissolved in water and inhaled nasally from an eyedropper; snorted; wiped on teeth, gums, and tongue.

PCP (phencyclidine)

Why kids like it: The drug produces a sense of distance and estrangement and, at times, an intense hallucinogenic state full of colors and sounds.

How it hurts kids: Because the drug blocks pain receptors, self-inflicted injury is common during violent PCP episodes. Chronic use will cause permanent brain damage, including impaired memory and speech. Paranoia as well as homicidal episodes are frequent. Violence is common. Other mood disorders such as anxiety and depression are also common. When large doses are consumed, convulsions, coma, heart and lung failure, and ruptured blood vessels in the brain can kill the user. Psychiatric treatment is often needed when PCP psychosis sets in. Someone on PCP should never be left alone.

What kids call it: PCP, phencyclidine, angel dust, love boat, lovely, hog, killer weed.

Forms kids use: Tablets, rock crystal, white powder, and liquid.

How kids use it: Injected; taken orally; smoked when sprayed on cigarettes, marijuana joints, or parsley; snorted.

LSD (lysergic acid diethylamide)

Why kids like it: Ingestion produces hallucinations and a trip that kids hope will be exhilarating rather than terrifying.

How it hurts kids: Bad trips can result in self-destructive behavior, severe panic, confusion, suspicion, anxiety, and loss of control. Flashbacks can cause a repeat of the destructive consequences. Organic brain damage can also result from heavy use.

What kids call it: LSD, acid, acid green, red green, white lightning, blue heaven, sugar cubes, microdot.

Forms kids use: Blotter paper or stamps impregnated with the chemical, a thin square of gelatin, clear liquid, brightly colored tablets.

How kids use it: Orally: licked off paper, placed in the eyes (liquid), eaten in gelatin form, dissolved in a beverage, placed on a sugar cube and eaten; sometimes it is placed in eyedropper bottles and dropped on the tongue.

Designer Drugs (Ecstasy, analogs)

Why kids like it: These drugs produce exhilarating feelings of warmth and confidence. Hallucinogenic effects are sometimes experienced.

How it hurts kids: Because these are analogs, or molecular derivatives, of chemicals such as PCP, amphetamines, Fentanyl, and Meperidine, all the dangers of the original chemicals are inherent in these drugs, but they also have an added unpredictability. Permanent brain damage is noted in many users. Overdose is common because the drug's strength is unpredictable. Users may also experience symptoms similar to those of Parkinson's disease, such as uncontrollable tremors, drooling, impaired speech, and paralysis. Addiction is frequent.

What kids call it: MDA, MDMA, Eve, MMDA, Ecstasy, MDEA, MPTP, MPPP, PEPAP, XTC, TMA, STP, PMA, DOB, E-tabs, X.

Forms kids use: White or white-gray powder, capsules, and tablets.

How kids use it: Orally, injected, and inhaled through the nose.

Mescaline, Peyote, Psilocybin, and Other Hallucinogens
Why kids like it: The chemical is ingested in search of a pleasant, illusionary trip of bright colors and intensified sounds.

How it hurts kids: Bad trips cause panic, confusion, suspicion, anxiety, total loss of control, destructive and suicidal behavior. Long-term use can produce organic brain damage such as memory impairment, confusion, and difficulty with abstract thinking. Psychotic behaviors are common.

What kids call it: Mesc, buttons, cactus, magic mushrooms, mushrooms, shrooms, STP, DMT.

Forms kids use: Tablets, capsules, hard brown disks; fresh or dried whole, chopped, or ground brown mushrooms.

How kids use it: Tablets and capsules are taken orally; disks are chewed, swallowed, or smoked; mushrooms are often mixed with other food and eaten or brewed as a tea.

More Than Meets the Eye

In addition to helping your children realize the hazards of the preceding list of drugs, you can help them understand the principle described at the beginning of chapter 5: What you see is not always what you get. Something that on the surface looks highly appealing may prove to be a source of great pain.

In the case of crack cocaine, for instance, what many people see is an intense high, which is available and affordable to almost everyone. A pusher turns on a kid, promising the good life, the opportunity to make his or her own decisions and be captain of his or her own ship. The naive child doesn't see crack for what it really is. The pusher is an advertiser for a drug cartel making millions of dollars by getting kids hooked. What the child sees is a beautiful, white powder offering instant pain relief and euphoria. What isn't seen is that the same substance also has the power to kill through overdose, heart failure, and suicide. And the lives it doesn't take will be destroyed in other ways, perhaps through dropping out of school, the loss of jobs, and the breaking up of relationships.

Talk to those on death row who have killed in the depths of depression once the crack high wore off. They will tell you to look beyond the hype and consider the consequences.

Education Is Key

If children can learn to think things through for themselves, they will possess a great drug prevention tool, particularly if they learn the key principle that what you see is not always what you get. Examples of this principle are all around us. I (Steve) once ordered a wave machine out of a catalog that guaranteed to make my house sound like the ocean. Instead it sounded like pure radio static, and my wife, Sandy, made me send it back. Products rarely deliver what the ads promise. Barbie dolls always come with the clothes sold separately. You don't get the full wardrobe shown on television. And GI Joe can never do as many tricks as the ads show.

Appearances are not reality in the programs on television either. What you see on television is rarely what you see in real life. Kids watch a half-hour sitcom or an episode of so-called "reality TV," and they see a world where every conflict is completely and perfectly resolved in less than an hour. That kind of scenario looks promising to someone who's growing up in a dysfunctional home. But real life is *not* what you get on television, in advertisements, by picking a bunch of leaves, or taking drugs.

The Essential Facts About Drug Abuse

Educating your children about drug abuse is simple. The essential facts are few:

- The use of any controlled substance not prescribed by a physician is drug abuse. Using any over-the-counter substance without adhering to the manufacturer's directions is also drug abuse. In 90 percent of the cases with kids, any drug use is drug abuse.

- The use of prescription medications, even when prescribed by a physician, is drug abuse in the following cases: a) when false symptoms are presented to manipulate a prescription from the physician; b) when the drug is used to relieve discomfort that needs to be processed over time through various forms of therapy and spiritual decisions; c) when a physician prescribes a drug rather than taking the time to help with an emotional problem or refer a patient to someone who will; and d) almost always, when a prescription sleeping medication is used over a period greater than two months.

Kids also need to understand the following concepts:

- Adult drug abuse does not justify kids' use of drugs. Parents are wrong to use mood-altering chemicals, and that wrong should be recognized by kids.

- The glamorous portrayal of drugs in movies does not justify kids' use of drugs. Nothing in life is free. Drug use has a cost higher than the purchase price. That price is called consequences, which the movies rarely show.

- Behind every use of a chemical is pain. Drug use by other kids who demonstrate little evidence of problems does not justify their use. A person's outward appearance doesn't show what pain he or she is experiencing. This agony may come from feeling rejected, from low self-esteem, from a broken home, or from a thousand other sources. The pain can be physical, mental, or emotional.

No one does drugs just for the fun of it. That is what users want to believe, and that is what the media often portray. But it is a lie. No matter what its cause, the pain is always there. People misuse drugs because they hurt, and the drugs are a way of treating that hurt.

Drug Abuse Is Never Justifiable

There is never a right reason for a child to abuse a chemical. Some people believe early experimentation with drugs is normal. But those who believe kids should be allowed to explore drugs deceive themselves and their children. Many times they are guilty parents who are reacting to their own past and inflicting their problems on their children. Remember: Kids who don't smoke or drink through their high school years are usually immune to the appeal of drugs later in life. On the other hand, those who experiment with drugs are the ones who go on to abuse them. The place to stop drug abuse is before it starts.

No Such Thing as "Experimental" Drug Use

One of the worst things that happened to our country was the acceptance of the lie that there is such a thing as recreational drug use. There is not. There is drug abuse and drug addiction. No third category exists.

If a person uses a drug long enough and often enough, he or she will become addicted. In the case of alcohol, about 20 percent of regular users become addicted. In the case of other drugs, about 90 percent of regular users become addicted. In the case of alcoholism, addiction usually occurs in the minority of users over a long period of time. In the case of crack cocaine, addiction occurs in the majority of users over a short period of time. This is why alcohol is legal and other substances are not; the risks are much greater with other drugs. This doesn't justify the use of alcohol, however. All the chemicals we have discussed in this book are addictive. To use any of them is risky. To use a drug such as crack cocaine is both risky and stupid.

Follow the Leader

The other day, as I (Steve) watched some children play follow the leader, I realized that everyone in the world knows how to play that game. You don't need to be taught the rules. They are inbred. When a leader starts playing, people instinctively start following. Then I realized we never stop playing the game. We follow some leader all our lives. It might be money, career, or a close friend whose approval we desire. So it is important to be careful in choosing a leader. Help your children select the right one.

As a parent, *you* serve as a powerful leader to your kids. Be sure you aren't leading by using old attitudes about a new challenge. The drug and alcohol problems of previous generations are not the same as those of our kids today. Don't make the mistake of thinking that because you lived through it, your children certainly will also.

The Lord's Leadership Style

Two thousand years ago, Jesus Christ came in the flesh and told us to follow Him. In Matthew 4:19, on seeing Peter at the Sea of Galilee, Jesus' first words to him were, "Come, follow me." The last words He spoke to Peter were, "Follow me!" (See John 21:19.) Jesus wants us likewise to follow Him. No child ever followed Christ to do drugs. No child ever followed Christ into drunkenness.

If you've decided to take the time to teach your children about drugs and alcohol, don't forget the most important lesson of all: Teach your children to follow Christ. If they learn to live as He lived, their adolescent years will be free of irresponsibility, drunkenness, and drugs. But we must return to the beginning of the education process. No greater teaching tool—for good or for ill—can be found than personal example. If you are not following Christ, your children will have a difficult time learning how to follow Him. If you are daily trying to follow Christ, however, you are teaching the lesson that forms the best foundation for prevention.

Chapter 8

Steroids, Diet Pills, HIV and AIDS: Is Your Child at Risk?

"Yes! I can't believe I can *finally* wear these jeans!"

Christina had never been more excited. For as long as she could remember, she had struggled with her weight. But now, standing alone in front of a dressing room mirror at the trendiest clothing store in the mall, she had achieved her goal.

"I *knew* I could do it! Boys can't say no to a girl who can wear size 0."

Somewhere around the age of five, Christina learned the truth. Her sister, Megan, was super-skinny...and cute...and popular. It always seemed like Megan's teachers liked her better...and she always had more friends—especially *boyfriends.* Christina, on the other hand, wasn't skinny—or at least not as skinny as her sister. So when she heard about the "Diet 0" pill that all the hot, young, Hollywood actresses were taking, Christina knew she had to try it.

And it worked. Christina went from a size 8 to a size 0 in less than a month. But that's not the only transformation Christina underwent that year. The honor student and sprinter who stood 5 feet 5 inches tall and weighed 115 pounds during the last track season weighed just 87 pounds when she was admitted to a clinic helping girls recover from eating disorders.

The Perfect Physique

Christina is not a real person...but her story illustrates how damaging some of the dietary supplements on the market can be. She represents the thousands of teen and preteenage girls who took some form of weight loss medication last year. Young women often start abusing diet pills during the most formative years of their lives. As a result, they run the risk of permanently stunting their growth in key areas—cardiopulmonary and reproductive organs being the primary risk targets.

The desire to develop and then maintain the "perfect body" is often the primary motivator for the abuse of diet pills. And it's not just girls who are involved in athletics, dance, or cheerleading who use them. Teen and preteen girls are driven to stop at nothing to have just the right look, which sometimes results in unhealthy eating patterns. Some girls will literally starve themselves, eating less than 300 calories per day. Others will allow themselves the emotional pleasure of experiencing the taste of food in their mouths, only to eliminate it (vomiting) before it can be properly digested. This cycle of "binging and purging" leaves a young girl severely malnourished and emotionally scarred.

The Dangers of Increased Metabolism

The use of dietary supplements is nothing new. Used properly, they increase the body's metabolism during a workout to maximize gains in muscle mass while decreasing the amount of fat stored in the body. So-called "low carb" diets help to facilitate this change by utilizing the combination of increased amounts of protein in the system coupled with a decrease (if not total elimination) of carbohydrate intake. In the short run, such a diet *will* lead to weight loss. But over time this is *not* a healthy course of action. That's where the diet supplements come in.

When the body generates heat, it uses energy to do so. This process is referred to as "burning calories." The hotter you get, the more calories you burn. Many dieters—especially bodybuilders—turn to products called thermogenics to "turn up the heat." A potent thermogenic dietary supplement will cause all of the body's internal furnace mechanisms to heat up. As a result, the body will expend even more calories than it would without the supplement. Used properly, this can lead to pleasant results. However, not everyone has the genetic makeup to be able to tolerate numerous doses of a thermogenic. As a result, the products can sometimes cause the body's metabolic "furnace" to keep running at the increased capacity well over the completion of training.[1]

Ephedrine is another over-the-counter stimulant that contributes to weight loss because of its thermogenetic effects. Because it speeds up the body's metabolic rate, fatty acids are released from the stored fat cells and the transition from fat to energy is increased. It also increases muscular stamina and endurance for bodybuilders. And yet it can also alter the psyche in such a way that an individual might become overly aggressive or anxious. You can imagine what kind of impact that could have on an adolescent whose emotional makeup can be a bit turbulent on occasion.[2]

Most of us adults would agree that the concept of having our metabolisms working in "high gear" 24 hours a day sounds exhausting and probably isn't healthy. But a number of teen and preteen guys and gals are seemingly willing to take that risk. They're experiencing a total reshaping of their bodies in increasing numbers—all thanks to "Clen."

Clenbuterol's Effect on Girls

When asked about their recent rapid weight loss, many Hollywood stars will pay homage to their personal trainers. Others thank their parents for blessing them with the "high metabolism genes" they inherited. But behind the scenes, agents and publicists are singing the praises of the medical professionals who figured out that bodybuilders, runway models, and actresses can all benefit from a medication that was designed to treat asthma in horses.

Clenbuterol—also known simply as "Clen"—is surprisingly easy to buy over the Internet. It is used and abused by guys looking to bulk up and gals dying to slim down. Here's how it works.

Clenbuterol is a long-acting agent that increases the body's temperature and heart rate, which helps burn fat. Where the danger lies is in how long Clen stays in your system. Where some supplements sweat out fairly easily during the course of a workout, Clenbuterol typically remains in the system for up to 24 hours. As a result, the increase in body temperature and heart rate continue for nearly one full day—even if you're not working out.

Many young actresses and models have discovered that Clen is a great way to experience short-term weight loss. No one is really sure the reason for the decline, but one thing is for certain: Most of the short-term weight loss Clen creates is often offset by long-term weight *gain.*

The risks of using an unproven medication like Clenbuterol far outweigh any positives. If you suspect your daughter might be using Clen for any reason, seek professional help immediately!

Boys Bulking Up

Girls aren't the only kids who struggle with the way they look. It's a battle for boys also. The primary difference, though, is that a young man often wrestles with a desire to develop a bigger, stronger body—almost the exact opposite of the so-called "perfect female form" of slender and sensual.

The influence of the visual media on television, movies, the Internet, and video games gives many a growing boy the impression that the "ultimate man" has countless muscles of steel. They see college football players and professional wrestlers with muscular structures that rival animated superheroes and wonder, "Why can't *I* look like that?" Well, by adding tons of protein to their diet and hitting the weight room as often as possible, such a look *can* be achieved. But using a diet supplement can kick-start their metabolism to ensure they'll get the look they want faster.

Boys also use Clenbuterol because it burns fat while building muscle mass. No one knows how the drug does this, so its effects aren't fully known. "Clen" is dangerous and should be avoided.

The Facts About Steroids

The stereotypical steroid user is a high school or college-age athlete, usually a football player or wrestler. He's looking to "bulk up" to gain a competitive edge against his competition. Trouble is, he's putting himself at tremendous risk by doing so.

Anabolic-androgenic steroids are man-made substances related to male sex hormones. (*Anabolic* refers to muscle-building; *androgenic* refers to increased masculine characteristics.) Used legally by prescription, these drugs can help treat conditions that occur when the body produces abnormally low amounts of testosterone. For example, a teenage boy who is slow in reaching puberty might benefit from limited, doctor-supervised treatments with anabolic steroids to spur on his growth.

In addition, patients experiencing the loss of lean muscle mass due to an illness such as AIDS can also benefit from steroid treatment. The trouble begins when teens and preteens begin using them *illegally*.

Side effects can include severe acne, tumors in the liver and kidneys, fluid retention, and high blood pressure. And though it might seem a bit cliché, the fact is that there *are* certain side effects which are gender-specific. In men, shrinking of the testicles, reduced sperm count, infertility, baldness, and the development of breasts are among the more common. For women, deepened voice, growth of facial hair, and changes in or the complete cessation of the menstrual cycle are known to take place.

Craig's Story

His desire was the same as most guys his age. Every time 18-year-old Craig walked in front of a mirror, he flexed his muscles. He wanted people to notice how large they were—or, as he used to say, he wanted to look "insanely huge—like an action figure."

Steroids weren't in the picture for Craig—at least not at first. Actually, he began working out because he needed to *lose* weight, approximately 20 pounds or so. But once the exercising began, the weight came off and was replaced with lean muscle—not the look Craig had been hoping for. So he increased the amount of lifting he did during his weight training and began experimenting with over-the-counter dietary supplements he purchased at a health food store. They gave him more of the look he desired, but now he wanted more bulk. So Craig joined the nearly 4 percent of all high school seniors who purchase illegal steroids over the Internet.[3]

Over the course of the next five years, the 5 foot 9-inch weight-lifter shot up to 225 pounds of steroid-enhanced muscle. But his increase in strength came at a high price—deteriorating health and ultimately hospitalization.

These days, Craig avoids steroids altogether, opting for a healthier lifestyle. He's glad he's a survivor instead of a statistic. Now he teaches other aspiring teen and preteen "muscle gods" about the dangers of anabolic-androgenic steroids.[4]

How Are Drug Abuse and HIV/AIDS Related?

Gina wasn't the most popular girl in school, but she certainly didn't lack for friends either. The 16-year-old was a decent student and held down a part-time job after school. She wasn't all that promiscuous either, which made her even more surprised when she learned that she tested positive for HIV.

"I don't have a steady boyfriend, and I don't sleep around," Gina protested. "I like to party sometimes with my friends. But I'm a *girl*. Isn't AIDS something only gay guys get?"

Apparently not. Gina is one of the growing number of teens and preteenage girls who are contracting HIV as a result of intravenous drug use.

What Are HIV and AIDS?

In the early 1980s, scientists first identified the Human Immu-nodeficiency Virus (HIV). They determined that it was capable of destroying a certain kind of white blood cell that is crucial to the normal function of the body's immune system. Without these white blood cells functioning at their peak, the immune system is compromised, unable to fend off even the most basic viral attacks.

HIV in its late stage is known as AIDS. The development of AIDS from HIV can take from several months to more than 17 years. People with Acquired Immune Deficiency Syndrome (AIDS), with treatment, can often live many years, but as of this writing there remains no known cure for this powerful, harmful virus.

What Causes HIV Infection?

The first cases of HIV and AIDS in the United States were diagnosed in patients who engaged in dangerous homosexual activity and intravenous drug use and abuse. Since the homosexual community was hit particularly hard by this malady during the early 1980s, many assumed that AIDS was exclusively a "gay disease." However, over the course of the next two decades, it became apparent that drug users were also at risk—especially teens.

When news of the disease first broke, many were led to believe that AIDS could be contracted simply by being in the same room with an infected person or by merely shaking his or her hand. We now know that HIV can be transferred among people if an infected person's blood and/or other bodily fluids come into contact with the blood, broken skin, or mucous membranes of an uninfected person. In addition, an expectant mother who has been infected with HIV can pass the virus on to her babies during pregnancy, delivery, and breastfeeding.

Drug abuse and addiction have been connected to the spread of HIV since the virus was first recognized. Most are familiar with the concept that "sharing dirty needles" and the intravenous nature of some forms of drug abuse make it a natural breeding ground for HIV. What is often overlooked, however, is the fact that noninjection drugs like "crack" cocaine also play a role in its spread. The addictive and intoxicating effects of many of these types of drugs can impair judgment to the point where young people—especially teens—engage in impulsive and unsafe behavior.

Behavior associated with drug use and abuse is now the single largest factor in the spread of HIV. Since the epidemic began, injection drug use has accounted for 36 percent of all AIDS cases in the U.S. and 25 percent worldwide. Gina may have been genuinely surprised to find out that her "recreational" drug use led to HIV infection, but the fact is that 39 percent of the women living with AIDS in the U.S. contracted the virus through injection drug use. (Heterosexual contact accounts for 42 percent of all the AIDS cases among American women.[5]

Good News?

In the nearly 30 years since HIV was first diagnosed, there is some hopeful news. Thanks to treatment known as HAART (highly active antiretroviral therapy), HIV is no longer the death sentence it once was. Even so, there are still around 40,000 new AIDS cases reported each year. The most recent estimates put the number of people living with HIV or AIDS in the United States at around 1 million. According to the Centers for Disease Control, nearly 40,000 young people ages 13 to 24 had been diagnosed with HIV through the end of 2003. That represents approximately 4 percent of all the AIDS cases reported in the U.S. at that time, but less than .1 percent of the total American teen population.[6]

There is increasing evidence suggesting that drug abuse treatment *can* help prevent the spread of HIV/AIDS among teens and preteenagers. Prevention and community-based outreach programs for at-risk kids play a large role in that process. If your son or daughter isn't classified as "at risk" or "high risk," don't relax. Middle and late adolescence is a time when kids are most likely to take risks in the first place. So just because your son or daughter has never done anything risky up to this point, don't think there isn't a possibility.

Kids who do not do drugs are still at risk of using unwise or unsafe sexual practices. During this season of life, they're given to acting on emotions and sometimes make decisions that far outweigh their maturity level. Make sure you initiate an ongoing dialog with your kids about sex and sexuality *before* they might put themselves in harm's way. The same holds true for drug and alcohol use and abuse. Drugs and alcohol can increase the chances of unsafe behavior so make sure your kids know the dangers.

THE SOLUTIONS

Chapter 9

Roadblocks and Building Blocks

Every 30 minutes in the United States:

- 29 kids will attempt suicide (ages 15 to 24)
- 24 teens will give birth out of wedlock (ages 10 to 19)
- 13 teenage girls will get abortions (ages 10 to 19)[1]
- 57 teens (ages 10 to 17) will commit an alcohol-induced assault[2]

When you multiply these statistics over a day, a week, a month, or a year it is easy to see that families are suffering. These kids are our neighbors, friends, and relatives, as well as members of our own families.

If we want to drug-proof our children, we must become students of the rapidly changing culture. Our children are being raised in a very different atmosphere from that facing any previous generation. One youth minister put it this way, "Yes, we were 8, 11, 13, and 15, but we were never their age." Our kids experience so much more so early in their lives. The average age of first drug use is now 13; of first alcohol use, 11. One in three fourth graders polled by the *Weekly Reader* reported feeling pressured by others to drink, and the figures increased steadily as the kids got older:

- Grade 4......35%
- Grade 5......39%
- Grade 6......49%

We were never their age!

The Revolution of Change

We don't mean to be alarmists. Some kids are choosing not to be involved in drug and alcohol abuse. Parents, however, must have the facts and do the best job possible to raise their children in healthy homes. In this chapter we will address two questions: 1) Why do kids act the way they act? and 2) What can we do to create a positive, drug-free environment?

Let's take a look at several potential roadblocks to sobriety in the society in which our young people live.

The Substance Abuse Revolution

Our children are growing up in a world offering mixed messages about drugs and alcohol. On the one hand, they hear that substance abuse is America's number one problem. Politicians, pastors, teachers, parents, and sports figures are working to stop this menace. Yet the drugs of choice are more readily available and stronger than ever before.

Those who choose to live by the little jingle they teach in kindergarten, "Be smart, don't start," will be in the minority. Alcohol remains the drug of choice among senior high school students, according to the annual National High School Senior Survey put out by the National Council on Alcoholism and Drug Dependence. According to the survey, 32 percent of seniors, 24 percent of tenth graders, and 8 percent of eighth graders reported being drunk during the past month.[3] Yes, drugs are at all children's doorsteps, and we cannot afford to say drug influence will never happen to them.

Media Revolution and Substance Abuse

On February 5, 2006, nearly 100 million people watched the Pittsburgh Steelers and the Seattle Seahawks do battle in Super Bowl XL, fighting it out for professional football's world championship.

It's somewhat ironic that many of the star athletes stood before the microphone to say "users are losers," and then what seemed like every other commercial (sold at 2.4 million dollars for a 30-second spot) was a beer commercial with the general theme that it's a "Good call!" for choosing their brand.

Kids receive not only a distorted picture of how much people drink, but they also receive almost uniformly positive images of alcohol—how it allegedly enhances sociability (back-slapping buddies tying one on in a bar) and magnifies sex appeal (starry-eyed lovers gazing at each other over a bottle of white wine).

We believe that TV and movies have a profound influence in making drugs and alcohol appealing to children. Many authorities today believe adolescents and young adults heavily exposed to television and print-media alcohol ads are more than twice as likely to perceive drinking as attractive, acceptable, and rewarding as those less exposed.

Sexual Revolution and Substance Abuse

Jackie was one of the leaders of my (Jim's) church youth group. She was raised in a wonderful Christian home and had parents who modeled their values in positive ways. As Jackie entered the natural experimental phase of her teenage years, she went to a few parties and drank a few beers. She told me she drank because of the peer pressure and simply out of curiosity.

One Saturday morning she showed up at Cathy's and my door. Her eyes were swollen and red; she had obviously been crying for hours. We brought her into our home and calmed her down, and then she told us an all-too-common story.

"I went to a party last night and, really for the first time, drank way too much. The next thing I knew, I was having sexual intercourse with a boy I hardly knew. I'm so embarrassed. I'm ashamed. I can't face my family or even God."

How many "Jackies" experience similar events every weekend? Today's young people are making sexual decisions based on: 1) peer pressure; 2) emotional involvement that exceeds their maturity level; 3) a lack of positive, healthy sex education; and 4) a lack of self-control because they are high on drugs or alcohol.

Materialism and Substance Abuse

In a recent youth group meeting I (Jim) attended, the kids told each other what they wanted to be or do when they "grew up." One ninth grader said, "I want to be rich."

I said, "Okay, but what do you want to be or do to become rich?"

"You don't understand," he said. "I don't care what I do. I just want to be wealthy. I want a house near the water, a boat, a sports car, and a life free of worry."

I said, "Sort of like the bumper sticker that reads, 'The person with the most toys wins.'"

"You got it," he replied.

My young friend was making the common mistake of thinking that money buys happiness. He was very wrong. Yet it is difficult to convince this generation of that truth.

A young man who was dragged into my office by his parents before he was ready for help said to me, "Can I be honest with you? I'm 18 years old. I make more money selling drugs than my father does in a job he hates. With all the money I'm making, I can stay high and happy." Today's young people have more disposable income than any previous generation, and they are spending it more and more on drugs and alcohol.

Peer Influence Revolution

Sociologists tell us that in the 1960s the greatest influence on teenagers was still their parents, but a major shift has taken place since then. Peers rival parents in their influence on our teenagers. This means we dare not underestimate the importance of knowing whom our children spend the most time with.

I (Steve) recently wrote a letter to my best friend from high school. His name is Cliff, and I thanked him for being the kind of person he was back then. He never suggested we use drugs of any sort. I count his strong support as a key factor in my never developing a drug problem. But too few kids today have a best friend such as Cliff. Too many kids have friends who want them to "just say yes."

A study of 8,000 high school students in the state of New York found peers extremely important in both introducing children to drugs and in reinforcing continued use. Of the students who reported no close friends who used marijuana, less than two percent themselves used drugs. Seventeen percent of those who said they had a "few" friends who used drugs were themselves drug users. Fifty percent of those who reported "some" of their friends were users had used drugs themselves.

The percentage of drug users continued to rise with the number of reported friends who were drug-oriented. Eighty percent of the students who said most of their friends were drug-oriented had used drugs themselves. Finally, of those who reported "all" their friends as drug-oriented, more than 90 percent admitted using drugs. This study also found that the number of weekly visits with friends who were drug-oriented had an influence on drug use.[4]

Our children will become like the friends with whom they spend the most time. Young people today live out their lives in "friendship clusters" of two or three best and most influential friends. If Sandy wears a certain style of clothes, so will Jamie and Brooklyn. If Jamie listens to heavy metal music, so will her best friends. If Brooklyn experiments with drugs, the odds are so will Sandy and Jamie.

Family Revolution and Substance Abuse

The best predictor of adolescent drinking habits is the attitude and behavior of parents toward alcohol. For example, children of alcoholics have a four-times-greater risk of developing alcoholism than children of nonalcoholics. Generally, children are more prone to abuse drugs if their parents:

- Smoke cigarettes
- Abuse alcohol or are alcoholics
- Take illicit drugs
- Use any substance to help master stress
- Impart an ambivalent or positive attitude toward illegal drugs[5]

Because alcoholism is on both sides of my (Jim's) family, I've made a conscious decision not to drink. I am concerned about my potential predisposition toward alcohol, but I'm more concerned about my children's predisposition. If my three girls see Daddy drink one harmless beer or glass of wine, they may think, *Well, Dad drinks, so it's okay for me to drink.*

The family medicine cabinet can also have a negative effect on children. If the kids see Mom rush to the medicine cabinet and say, "I feel so lousy I've got to get a Valium," it reinforces the idea that drugs make you feel better. It's much better to say, "I only take medicine when I'm sick." Never say you take medicine to make you "feel better." And if you haven't cleaned out the medicine cabinet for a while, now is the time!

According to a Manisses Communications Group survey, 20 percent of parents believe their children would drink over a holiday weekend. Thirty-nine percent of the teens said they intend to do so.[6]

Although four out of five parents in a Midwestern school district considered marijuana use to be a problem among seventh- through twelfth-graders, only one in five thought his or her child was involved.

Self-Esteem Revolution

The primary task of the preteen and teenager is to construct a self-identity. And let's face it: Most kids suffer from low self-esteem. They can easily be seduced by chemicals that make them feel good and medicate their pain. Why do kids have such poor self-esteem? They suffer for many reasons, but we would like to concentrate on a few of the most common.

Physical appearance. Young people are extremely anxious about their appearance. Although most often they want to be their own person and not look like Mom or Dad, they do want to look and dress like their dominant peer group.

A while ago a young girl quit coming to my (Jim's) youth group meetings. Her mother was sure the reason was drug abuse, and I thought she had some big spiritual problem. Finally Leslie, her mother, and I got together to talk. With fire in her eyes, glaring at her mother, she opened up and said, "I'll tell you why I don't go to this church anymore. It's because she won't buy me any Jordache jeans, and everybody wears Jordache but me." I almost wanted to laugh because my imagination had made this into a much bigger event. Yet, in Leslie's eyes, it was the most important issue of her life.

When I (Jim) was the only fourth-grade boy in my entire school who had hair under my arms, it was absolutely devastating. I cringed every time I had to raise my hand in class or play skins and shirts on the basketball court. My appearance didn't measure up to the cultural norm. By the time I was in eighth grade, I was wearing sleeveless shirts because I was now proud of that growth under my arms!

Losing by comparison. Another key roadblock to a good self-image is playing the comparison game. Adolescents invariably assess themselves relative to someone who is better looking, smarter, or more talented. The player never wins.

When I (Steve) worked with psychiatric patients in Fort Worth, Texas, I heard story after story of parents who had compared their kids with other children. Many of our patients were living with the belief that they could never meet their parents' expectations or their siblings' standards. They thought themselves inadequate and, thus, became totally inadequate to cope with life.

Sociologists call it self-fulfilling prophecy. If you believe you are ugly, you will be. If you believe you can't accomplish the task, you won't. (Fortunately, the opposite is also true.)

Distorted view of God. Many young people have a wrong view of God, and we are convinced this is a major factor in poor self-esteem. For a majority of young people, God is a great killjoy—He is a God of works and is slow to forgive. Young people see themselves only as guilty, condemned sinners unworthy of love and respect. From the spiritual perspective, their self-concept is entirely negative. The gospel to them is not good news, but bad news of condemnation.

Jesus said, "You will know the truth, and the truth will set you free" (John 8:32). We have found that only when young people really comprehend the unconditional love and forgiveness of God are they truly set free to be all God created them to be.

Is There Hope?

Given the realities of our culture and the overwhelmingly negative statistics, the questions in every parent's mind today are: Can I make a positive difference? Is there hope? Our answer? Yes!

I (Jim) was reminded recently of an old Sunday school lesson about David and Goliath (see 1 Samuel 17). David was sent to the battlefield by his father to check on his brothers and report back to him. When David got to the scene of conflict, he saw Goliath come out to the Israelites and call them to battle. Goliath's challenge was that if any Israelite would fight him and win, the Philistines would serve Israel. If Goliath won the battle, however, the people of Israel would become slaves of the Philistines.

But no Israelite had volunteered. When David observed this, he was incensed that Goliath would mock the living God, and he asked King Saul for permission to fight Goliath. David believed that with God's help, Israel would prevail. His perspective was certainly different from that of the others. He could have said, "Goliath is so big. I can't win!" Instead he said, "Goliath is so big—I can't miss!"

This is exactly the attitude we must have as we put together a plan to drug-proof our children. Yes, the culture is scary, and, frankly, we have struggles ahead of us. With God's help, however, and a deep desire to make a difference, we can prevail.

To that end, we have put together six building blocks to form a solid foundation for growth. You won't find any gimmicks or the latest parenting fad. These six blocks are what we have seen work through the years not only to keep kids drug free, but also to help them be a positive influence in the world.

Give Your Children Time and Attention

Perhaps the biggest problem in parenting today is the overcommitment and fatigue experienced by parents. Vince Lombardi, well-known coach and that "great theologian," once said, "Fatigue makes cowards of us all." I (Jim) know I am at my worst when I am overcommitted and tired. Cathy and I never imagined before we had children how much time it would take to raise them right.

It used to be that the average father of a teenager spent around 40 hours a week working, 50 hours sleeping, several hours dressing and grooming, but only 21 minutes *a week* talking with his son or daughter. Multiplied over a lifetime, you can see the problem: That father would wind up spending 25 years sleeping, 12 years working, 3 years grooming, and only 11 days, 16 hours talking with his child.[7]

There's been a change in parental attitudes in recent years—and we think it's a change for the better. The "new dad" is helping out more around the house, largely because he is home more often. Dads are now spending an average of 3.4 hours each workday at home when their kids are present.[8] This doesn't guarantee that the amount of time talking with their kids will automatically increase, but it does go a long way toward improving the odds.

When I (Jim) finished graduate school in Princeton, New Jersey, a friend gave me a card I have kept. It reads, "Jim, if the devil can't make you bad, he will make you busy." Many times I have looked at that card and considered it a guiding principle for my life. I don't want my children to grow up thinking of Dad only as busy.

Whether we like it or not, our schedules reveal our priorities. When we give our children time and attention, it means we are willing to listen to them. Listening is the language of love. Sometimes our kids don't immediately want the right answer as much as they want to know we are willing to take time to listen. They need to feel important.

I hear many busy fathers say they can't give their children a large quantity of time, so they give them quality time instead. But kids need quality *and* quantity time. They regard our very presence as one of the most significant signs of caring.

Paul made an important statement to all parents: "We loved you so much that we were delighted to share with you not only the gospel of God but our lives as well, because you had become so dear to us" (1 Thessalonians 2:8). Paul loved these people so much he gave them the gospel of God and his own life as well. When kids know beyond a shadow of a doubt that they have our attention, they feel secure.

Give Your Children Integrity

A great proverb to memorize is: "The man of integrity walks securely" (Proverbs 10:9). We would go a step further and say that if parents live lives of integrity, not only will they walk securely, but so will their children. Kids need parents who will be open and vulnerable and good models for living.

A mom, dad, and son were in my (Jim's) office because the son had a problem with lying. Dad was being hard on his son for stretching the truth. The conversation took a different turn, however, when the son said, "But wait, Dad. Last night when your boss called, you told me to tell him you weren't there. Isn't that a lie?"

My (Jim's) life was changed early in my ministry when I heard a tape by Dr. James Dobson entitled "You Can Save Your Marriage." He told his own story of an overcommitted travel and ministry schedule and his consequent decision to cut back and stay at home—to practice what he preached, so to speak. I so appreciated this man's integrity that I made a decision to change my workaholic lifestyle and make my family a priority. It has proved to be one of my best decisions.

We like this little conversation from Dr. David Elkind's book *The Hurried Child:*

> Child A: "My daddy is a doctor, and he makes a lot of money, and we have a swimming pool."
>
> Child B: "My daddy is a lawyer, and he flies to Washington and talks to the president."
>
> Child C: "My daddy owns a company, and we have our own plane."
>
> Child D proudly says: "My daddy is here."[9]

Another aspect of integrity is that when you love your spouse with an obvious commitment, your children will feel secure. Cathy and I (Jim) have noticed that when we do little things such as hugging or holding hands when we walk, our girls like it. We also tell them Mommy and Daddy have a weekly date night because we love each other very much and want to spend time together.

We realize not every parent has a spouse. If you *are* married, however, we can't emphasize enough the connection between secure children and healthy, loving marriages. Before some parents can put together a drug plan for their children, they may need to put together a "healthy marriage plan" for themselves.

Give Your Children Affirmation

Abraham Maslow, a psychologist, said, "It takes nine affirming comments to make up for each critical comment we give our children."

When I am frustrated with my children, I (Jim) find myself trying to produce in them guilt, fear, intimidation, or some other negative motivation. But what really changes children for the long term is affirmation and encouragement. This doesn't mean we don't confront negative behavior or enforce the rules of home. Affirmation, however, is a greater motivator for change than guilt or fear.

More than anything else, our children need to hear we believe in them. Jesus nicknamed Simon "Petras," or Peter. The correct translation is "the Rock." Jesus looked at Simon, an uneducated fisherman, and believed he would become the rock, or leader, of the Jerusalem church. Three years later, who was the recognized leader in Jerusalem? The man who had become what Jesus foresaw. Do your children know without a doubt that you believe in them?

We must look for ways to shower our children with praise. Mark Twain spoke for most of us when he said, "I can live two months on one good compliment." I (Jim) told our daughter Rebecca the other day, "You did a great job cleaning up your room."

Her reply was, "Thank you, Daddy. I love you." She thought for a moment and added, "I even like you."

All normal human beings respond to praise. We crave affirmation so much we will do almost anything to receive it. One friend put it this way, "Whoever gives your kids praise and attention has power over them." If you don't praise your children, someone else will, and that someone could be a drug dealer. Many people with lifestyles contrary to your own are willing to praise your kids to get what they want from them.

Give Your Children Opportunities to Communicate

"How was school?"

"Fine."

"Anything special happen today?"

"No."

"Is everything all right?"

"Yep."

"Jeannie, the phone's for you."

An hour later, because she hadn't seen her friend Linda for at least two hours and "there was so much to talk about," you have to tell Jeannie to get off the phone.

Communicating with kids is difficult work. Sometimes walking on water seems like it would be easier. No matter how frustrating it is, please don't give up. Do whatever it takes to keep the communication lines open. In the Burns' household, my children have special dates with Dad. For some reason, when Christy and I are sitting at McDonald's eating fast food to our heart's delight, good communication flows both ways. Our youngest, Heidi, responds when we go to the park.

A friend had been wanting to talk with his teenage son about God. He had tried at various times but struck out. Then one Saturday they spent the day together putting up a basketball hoop in the backyard. After they finished and had played a game of one-on-one, the son casually said, "Dad, I've been thinking about God lately, and I have some questions. Would you mind helping me understand a few issues?" They sat underneath the basketball hoop and had an outstanding conversation. The communication lines were open because they had spent time together.

Date nights, shopping sprees, games, and special trips are ways of enhancing the communication process. Everyone experiences a deep hunger to feel significant and have meaningful conversation. Parents who keep the communication lines open help prevent deep heartache later in life.

Give Your Children a Network

In 1940, approximately 65 percent of all households in America had at least one grandparent as a full-time, active member. By 1988, less than 2 percent of American homes had a grandparent living with them.[10] We are the first generation of Americans who are raising our children without a strong network of grandmas, grandpas, aunts, uncles, cousins, nephews, and close neighbors. Young people need a network of significant adults who will listen to them, take them seriously, and make them feel they are part of a caring community.

Both of us (Steve and Jim) are actively involved in the life of a church (we attend the same one), and we believe the church family can help meet our kids' need for a support network. In this mobile age, the church can be a rock of encouragement. We can't think of a better peer influence than a youth group where kids are developing the spiritual, mental, physical, and social areas of their lives in a positive environment.

Do your kids feel they have a network of significant others who can help them through their sometimes rocky path of development? If they don't have as solid a network as you would like, we strongly suggest that creating one becomes a high priority.

Give Your Children a Spiritual Foundation

This may sound corny to some, but the old adage is true: "The family that prays together stays together." Although studies show little difference in drug and alcohol use between Christian and non-Christian young people, one of the strongest factors in deciding not to abuse drugs in all the studies we came across was an active spiritual life. The more involved kids were with their faith, the better the chances they would refrain from drug abuse.

Tim and Donna were cousins and members of our youth group. Their families came from the same socioeconomic group, and both families were active in the church and community. Tim and Donna attended about the same number of youth group events. By the time Tim graduated from high school, however, he had left the church and was heavily involved in drugs. Donna, on the other hand, remained active in the church and drug free.

What made the difference? Tim was a spectator. His friendships and extracurricular activities all took place outside the church. Donna's social life was centered in the church. She dated boys in the group, participated in missions trips, and even volunteered to stuff envelopes.

We cannot overemphasize that kids become like the people who most influence them. That is why we believe active involvement in the church is such an important part of a drug-proof plan.

What can parents do to build a solid spiritual foundation in their children? Nothing is more significant than modeling the desired behavior in your own life. If your children see you possessing an active spiritual life, the odds are high they will follow suit. If you come off as "too holy" or never admit your weaknesses, their spiritual growth will be impaired.

A strong spiritual foundation needs to be built on the following principles: 1) God loves you unconditionally; 2) you are created in God's image; 3) you are a child of God; and 4) in Jesus Christ, your sins are forgiven. Let's look at each of these principles in a little more detail.

God loves kids unconditionally. We must help young people understand that God loves them not for what they do but for who they are. Because our society is so conditional, most young people—including those who have a church background—still do not believe God's love is unconditional and sacrificial. The message of Paul to the Romans is still the word for today: "But God demonstrates his own love for us in this: While we were still sinners, Christ died for us" (Romans 5:8).

God created kids in His image. Kids need to know they are a creation of God. Ephesians 2:10 says, "For we are God's workmanship, created in Christ Jesus to do good works, which God prepared in advance for us to do." The word "workmanship" can be translated from the original Greek to mean "poetry." So every person is a special work of God's poetry.

Kids who can say no to drugs, sexual promiscuity, and other temptations are kids who understand that they are God's poetry—unique, gifted, and different from every other person because God created each of us from a different mold.

They are children of God. Through Jesus Christ, we can approach the God of the universe and call Him Father. We need to help our children understand they are children of God and have all the rights and privileges of any other child of God. In the next chapter, we will discuss in-depth why kids take drugs, but one of the major reasons is that they need a sense of belonging. We can help them greatly by teaching that God takes care of His children and wants only the best for them. Here is an excellent biblical principle young people need to hear often:

Ask, and you will be given what you ask for. Seek, and you will find. Knock, and the door will be opened. For everyone who asks, receives. Anyone who seeks, finds. If only you will knock, the door will open. If a child asks his father for a loaf of bread, will he be given a stone instead? If he asks for fish, will he be given a poisonous snake? Of course not! And if you hardhearted, sinful men know how to give good gifts to your children, won't your Father in heaven even more certainly give good gifts to those who ask him for them? (Matthew 7:7-11 TLB).

Kids are forgiven. Forgiveness is available for the asking. We like to tell kids, "God is absentminded when it comes to confessed sin." What we mean is that He forgives and forgets. "If we confess our sins, he is faithful and just and will forgive us our sins and purify us from all unrighteousness" (1 John 1:9). We are new creations in Christ (see 2 Corinthians 5:17). No longer do we need to be accepted by a crowd because God has accepted us as His children *and* forgiven our sins. And His forgiveness is forever.

I (Jim) wish you could meet Linda. Today she is a radiant mother of three beautiful children. She has a good marriage, an active spiritual life, and more enthusiasm for life than just about anyone I know. But life wasn't always so wonderful for her.

Linda was an illegitimate child and was raised in an abusive home. By the time she was in ninth grade, she had lost her virginity and drugs and alcohol were regular habits. When I met her she was a high school student. She said, "Life is going nowhere for me, and I've made some very wrong decisions."

Over a period of time, we became good friends. We talked about her background and how her abuse as a child was not her fault. We spoke of hope and change. One evening she said, "But what about all the sin that was my own decision? I can't blame everything on my past."

I explained the essence of the gospel of Jesus Christ and told her, "The old Linda can be buried, and in Christ's love and forgiveness you can be a brand-new person."

Her smile was hesitant, but she said, "Okay, I'm willing to try."

We prayed together, thanking God for His forgiveness. When we finished, she looked the same on the outside, but on the inside she was different. And by God's grace, she hasn't looked back. She now lives free from the guilt and shame that once permeated her life.

Every recovering alcoholic and drug addict we have worked with has had to come to three important realizations. Only when that person accepts these does he or she begin recovery. When a person accepts these principles early, addiction can be avoided altogether. The first realization is that he or she cannot manage life alone. The second is that God can. The third is that he or she must *allow* God to manage his or her life.

The addict must become involved in the spiritual pilgrimage that all of life should be. Of the six building blocks, the spiritual foundation is the most important. When a spiritual foundation is missing, drugs and alcohol will be used to fill the void. A solid, Christian, spiritual foundation of the drug-proof child wards off or even prevents the void from ever developing. Help your child build a foundation that will last a lifetime.

Chapter 10

Identifying Chemical Abuse in Your Kids

A family was concerned about their 16-year-old daughter. Her behavior was unpredictable, and her attitude was terrible. The parents had smelled alcohol on her breath a couple of times recently. They brought her to me (Steve) to help prevent an alcohol problem from developing. But after a couple of hours of getting to know each other, it became apparent that we were too late for prevention. This young girl had been a practicing alcoholic since the age of 12, and her parents had never suspected it.

My task was to help them face the problem they had refused to see, although many indicators had been evident besides those two times of alcohol on her breath. It was hard for them, as it is for any parents, to admit chemical addiction in their own child. Parents' lack of knowledge about their own children is common.

There is a large discrepancy between the number of kids who use drugs and the number of parents who think their kids use them. The belief that it could never happen to them prevents parents from seeing or acknowledging their children's involvement in drugs or alcohol (see the chart on the next page). But parents who deny reality keep their kids from getting needed help. That is why it's best to watch for the problem rather than expect that your children will escape using drugs. If you are not looking for it, you often won't find it. And if you don't know what to look for, you certainly won't find it early.

Parents Underestimate Drug Usage

Parents underestimate their kids' drug and alcohol use, according to an Emory University School of Medicine survey. The researchers asked 402 seniors if they had used various substances in the last 30 days. Parents were asked if they thought the seniors had used the same substances in the last 30 days. Parents estimated alcohol and drug usage consistently lower than actual senior usage.

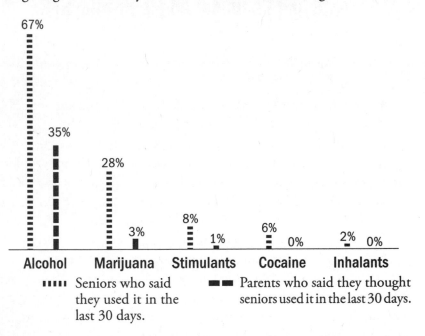

This chapter is designed to help you identify an abuse problem as early as possible. The sooner drug or alcohol use is detected and action is taken, the better the chances for changing behavior. First, we'll present some generalities about kids who stay sober. If your children are not using drugs, the following will usually be true:

- You are able to communicate with your children. Few barriers prevent either of you from expressing your feelings or ideas. Your children want to hear your opinions.

- You know and approve of your children's friends. They are not mysterious characters who never come around. They participate in some of your family events such as meals or trips. You are their friends, too.

- Your children perform adequately and consistently in school. They may not be geniuses, but they have few failures and many successes. Attendance is not a problem, and their teachers like having them in class.

- Your kids are involved in healthy activities outside of school. Their interests are varied, and new things are accepted as challenges. They are not stuck in a rut, always doing the same things with the same people. They probably enjoy church groups.

- Your children smile, laugh, and are involved with the family. They have their private spaces, but they exhibit little suspicious behavior. Sulking while alone is rare.

- The way your kids dress may not be what you would choose, but they are fairly clean and neat. Their clothing certainly is not the most radical dress of anyone in school, and it is free of drug paraphernalia and images.

- Your children have the ability to say no. You can recall several times when you've heard them turn down invitations. They usually don't let friends talk them into things they really don't want to do. They have relatively strong self-esteem.

- Your kids are honest with you. You rarely catch them in a lie, and if you do, it is about a minor matter. What you hear about your children from others is consistent with what you know about them.

- Your children's moods are relatively stable. You rarely see large swings from intense anxiety to deep depression.

- Your kids openly communicate a consistent message that they don't do drugs, their friends don't do drugs, and they disapprove of doing drugs. When they discuss others who abuse drugs, it is with sadness.

Your children, although drug and alcohol free, won't exhibit all ten traits. No child is perfect, and no cookie cutter fits every adolescent. But an abstinent young person will exhibit most of these traits.

What about the child involved with drug experimentation or regular use? The signs are often subtle and can be confused with normal adolescence. But when the signs continue to surface, you can be assured it is not an adolescent adjustment problem. It is probably alcohol or other drugs.

Identifying the Danger Signs

If we have heard it once, we have heard it a thousand times from shocked parents: "We had no idea our (son or daughter) was using drugs. Sure his lifestyle had changed, but we assumed it was typical teenage behavior." People who work with drug and alcohol addicts every day can see the problem much easier than parents can. Parents seem to be the last to know. So sometimes it's good to get a second opinion.

A wonderful couple came to me (Jim) concerned about their daughter's drop in grades. They were afraid she had a learning disability. I asked general questions about the girl's behavior, and after hearing their answers I said, "I don't want to dismiss the possibility of a learning disorder, but I would bet my life's savings (not much on a youth minister's salary!) your daughter has a drug or alcohol problem. The signs and symptoms all fall into place."

Both parents stood up, thanked me for my time, and informed me I was absolutely wrong. Two months later their daughter entered treatment for acute alcoholism.

Subtle Symptoms

The following symptoms could point to problems other than drug abuse. But they all indicate problems needing professional treatment. If every symptom describes your child, immediate action should be taken. If only a few of the symptoms are present, they could be common aspects of the teenage years. We suggest you at least discuss your concerns with your child.

- Secrecy
- Change in friends

- Change in dress and appearance
- Increased isolation
- Change in interests or activities
- Drop in grades
- Getting fired from an after-school job
- Changes in behavior around home
- Staying out all night
- Possession of a bottle of eyedrops (to counter blood-shot eyes)
- Sudden change in diet that includes sweets and junk food (many drugs give the users cravings or "munchies")
- Dropping out of sports participation

Not-So-Subtle Symptoms

The following symptoms indicate chemical abuse. If several of these symptoms are present in your child, you should take action immediately before the problem develops into addiction.

- Deep depression accompanied by hours of extra sleep
- Depression
- Extreme withdrawal from the family
- Increased, unexplained absenteeism from school
- Little or no involvement in church activities
- Increase in mysterious phone calls that produce frantic reactions
- Starting smoking
- Money problems
- Extreme weight loss or gain
- Appearance of new friends older than your child
- Expulsion from school
- Rebellious and argumentative behavior
- Listening to heavy metal rock or rap music with pro-drug lyrics

- Acting disconnected or "spacey"
- Physically hurting younger siblings
- Attempting to change the subject or skirt the issue when asked about drug or alcohol use
- Changing the word "party" from a noun to a verb
- Discussing times in the future when he or she will be allowed to drink legally
- Long periods of time in the bathroom
- Burnt holes in clothes and furniture

Surefire Indicators of Chemical Abuse

When the following signs are noticeable, you should have no question in your mind that your child is abusing drugs or alcohol. These are signals that the problem has not just started but has been in existence for some time. And you see only the tip of the iceberg. Most of the problem and its symptoms have been carefully hidden away so you won't intervene. But intervene is what you must do.

- Paraphernalia found in the bedroom: strange vials, small bags (a full box of bags would be an indicator that the child is also selling drugs), mirrors, pipes, tubes, razor blades, cigarette papers, foil, butane lighters, scales, matches, pop cans that have been converted into pipes (these will have a strange odor and fine holes on the side), bongs, roach clips, eyedrop containers (these could indicate that the child is storing LSD or some other drug in them), sneak-a-tokes (these are pipes that are disguised in color and shape as a cigarette)
- Possession of large amounts of money (indicates your child doesn't just use drugs, but is probably selling them to other kids as well)
- Needle marks on the arms or clothing that prevents you from seeing the arms
- Valuables disappearing from the house
- Arrests due to alcohol- or drug-related incidents

- Bloodshot eyes frequently
- Uncontrollable bursts of laughter with no apparent reason
- A runny or itchy nose that is not attributable to allergies or a cold (a red nose would also be an indicator)
- Dilated or pinpoint pupils
- Puffy or droopy eyelids that partially hang over the iris
- Mention of suicide or an attempt at suicide
- Disappearance or dilution of bottles in the liquor cabinet
- Time spent with people you know use drugs or alcohol
- Medicine disappearing from the medicine cabinet
- Defending peers' right to use drugs or alcohol

Several problems other than chemical abuse can produce similar symptoms. An anorexic or deeply depressed person could have some of the preceding signs. But if these symptoms are present, you need to act now. Intervention is required. Don't let the symptoms escalate. Don't assume your child is just going through a stage.

As your suspicions mount, your child's awareness of these suspicions will also increase. So delay does no good. Discuss the problem with your spouse, seek professional help, and develop a plan of action. The worst thing you can do is react quickly in anger. Contain yourself until you have sought professional help so you can plan an intervention program that is best for your child.

Drug Tests for Your Kids

When I (Steve) go to a doctor, no matter what my reason for being there, the doctor usually takes a urine sample and performs other minor tests so he can detect any problem he might not otherwise spot. I never had a doctor do routine urine tests before I went to Dr. Baylor. But he gave me an idea for a great way parents and their physicians can monitor kids' use of drugs.

If you have teenagers, it is a good idea to take them to the doctor at least twice a year for checkups. And when you do, make it standard procedure for your doctor to request a urine sample. Then be sure the doctor does a drug test. Tell your kids ahead of time that the doctor runs drug tests on all adolescents at every checkup. This way your kids will see it is not just you but also the doctor who is ensuring they have no drug problem.

If this testing is done from an early age, it won't cause conflict between you and your children. And if you actually suspect drug use, you can have the doctor perform a more extensive test.

Drugs are a monumental problem, and fighting them requires some extreme measures. Having a urine screening test performed is a simple way for you to learn if your kids are in trouble. It also provides a way out for children faced with pressure to use drugs. They can tell their friends that their parents will find out because the doctor tests their urine.

Parents' Reactions to Children's Drug Problems

Because of your love for your children and the natural urge to deny problems, you may have difficulty dealing with a drug or alcohol problem if it does occur. You may have become codependent yourself, making denial and compensation parts of your lifestyle. By comparing your life to the symptoms of codependency in the following list, perhaps you can determine whether your behavior fits the pattern of others who deny their loved one's problem or allow it to continue. If you see yourself in these descriptions, you need to seek professional help for yourself as well as for your kids.

- Trying to cover up children's irresponsible behavior rather than discussing it openly with a spouse, school personnel, or a friend
- Feeling that no matter how hard you try, you can do nothing to change your children's behavior
- Spending an inordinate amount of time talking to your children about problems and pleading for change
- Always questioning what you do and say, thinking

that if you change, your kids might be motivated to change

- Giving money to your kids behind your spouse's back
- Spending a large part of your day worrying about the kids and their problems
- Regularly sacrificing for your children, always putting their needs before your own
- Feeling a growing need to control your kids' behavior (rather than release them to greater independence)

Measuring Your Level of Codependency

If you can't see the problem in your children, perhaps you can see yourself in the pattern of codependency. If so, you are not alone. Millions of parents do all the wrong things for the right reasons. Love is powerful, especially for our children. But that love can be blind to your children's need for help, allowing the chemical addiction to progress. If you find yourself enabling the problem rather than stopping it, help is available. Getting help for yourself is the best step in moving toward an ultimate solution. When you stop enabling, you are ready to intervene and save your kids' lives.

One of the most effective ways to identify drug and alcohol abuse is with "an assessment." The following is an assessment tool for your use.

Questions for Parents

You may suspect your children are having trouble with alcohol or other drugs, but short of smelling liquor on their breath or discovering pills in their pockets, how can you tell for sure? Although symptoms vary, some tip-offs are common. Your answers to the following questions will help you determine if your children have drug or alcohol problems.[1]

1. Have your children's personalities changed markedly? Do they change moods quickly, seem sullen, withdraw

from the family, display sudden anger or depression, or spend hours alone in their rooms?

Yes____   No____   Uncertain____

2. Have your kids lost interest in school, school activities, or school athletics? Have their grades dropped at all?

Yes____   No____   Uncertain____

3. Have your children stopped spending time with old friends? Are they now spending time with kids who worry you? Are they secretive or evasive about who their friends are, where they go, and what they do?

Yes____   No____   Uncertain____

4. Are you missing money or other objects from around the house (money needed for alcohol and drugs), or have you noticed that your children have more money (possibly from selling drugs) than you expect?

Yes____   No____   Uncertain____

5. Have your kids tangled with the law in a situation involving drugs in any way? (You can be sure that if this has happened, there have been other times—probably many—when they have been drinking or using drugs but have not been caught.)

Yes____   No____   Uncertain____

6. Do your children get angry and defensive when you talk about alcohol and drugs, or do they refuse to discuss the topic at all? (People who are defensive about alcohol and drugs are often hiding how much they use.)

Yes____   No____   Uncertain____

7. Do you think you are not getting straight answers about your children's whereabouts, activities, and companions? (A young person may also lie about matters that seem unrelated to alcohol or drugs.)

Yes____   No____   Uncertain____

8. Have you smelled alcohol on your kids' breaths? Have you smelled marijuana on their clothing or in their rooms? (Slurred speech, unclear thinking, swaggering gait, bloodshot eyes, dilated pupils, and imprecise eye movement may also be indicators.)

   Yes____   No____   Uncertain____

9. Have your children lost interest in previously important hobbies, sports, or other activities? Have they lost motivation, enthusiasm, and vitality?

   Yes____   No____   Uncertain____

10. Have you ever found a hidden bottle, beer cans left in the car, marijuana seeds, marijuana cigarettes, cigarette rolling papers, drug paraphernalia (pipes, roach clips, stash cans, etc.), capsules, or tablets?

    Yes____   No____   Uncertain____

11. Have your children's relationships with you or other family members deteriorated? Do your kids avoid family gatherings? Are they less interested in siblings? Do they verbally (or even physically) abuse younger siblings?

    Yes____   No____   Uncertain____

12. Have your children ever been caught with alcohol or other drugs at school or at school activities?

    Yes____   No____   Uncertain____

13. Have your kids seemed sick, fatigued, or grumpy (possibly hungover) in the morning after drug or alcohol use was possible the night before?

    Yes____   No____   Uncertain____

14. Has your children's grooming deteriorated? Do they dress in a way associated with drug or alcohol use? Do they seem unusually interested in drug- or alcohol-related slogans, posters, music, or clothes?

    Yes____   No____   Uncertain____

15. Have your kids' physical appearances changed? Do they seem unhealthy, lethargic, more forgetful, or have a shorter attention span than before?

    Yes___   No___   Uncertain___

This questionnaire is not a scientific instrument and is not meant to definitively diagnose chemical abuse problems. Rather, the questions are "red flag" indicators, and your answers may show a need for further action. Keep in mind that "yes" answers to some of these questions may reflect normal adolescent behavior. Affirmative answers to questions directly relating to alcohol and drug use (questions 5, 8, 10, and 12) are, of course, special cause for concern. They indicate your children are almost certainly abusing chemicals, and action should be taken.

In general, you should look for an emerging pattern. A couple of "yes" or "uncertain" answers should alert you to suspect alcohol and drug use, monitor the children more closely, talk to knowledgeable sources, and prepare to seek help.

If you answered "yes" to three or more questions, help is probably needed now. Your children may be in the experimental stages, if not heavily involved. Remember, it is difficult to handle this problem without the help of professionals. This is not usually a problem that passes with time, and it may well be a life-or-death matter. If you are concerned, take action! Call a knowledgeable source such as a school counselor, other drug counselors who deal with adolescents, your local council on alcoholism or another drug–alcohol agency, and discuss this questionnaire.

Student Information

Most young people have used alcohol in one form or another, but few recognize alcoholism as a disease that can affect the young as well as the old. Ask your children to take the following short test; it may tell them something about themselves. Consider telling them you don't need to see the results; that this is an opportunity for them to evaluate their lives and see if they need help.

YES NO

— — 1. Do you lose time from school because of drinking?

— — 2. Is it necessary for you to drink to have fun?

— — 3. Do you drink in order to build up your self-confidence?

— — 4. Do you drink alone?

— — 5. Is drinking affecting your reputation? Do you care?

— — 6. Do you drink to escape from school or home worries?

— — 7. Do you feel guilty after drinking?

— — 8. Does it bother you if someone says you drink too much?

— — 9. Do you sneak drinks from your parents' liquor supply or anyone else's?

— — 10. Do you generally "make out" better when you drink?

— — 11. Do you get into financial trouble buying liquor?

— — 12. Do you feel a sense of power when you drink?

— — 13. Have you lost friends since you started drinking?

— — 14. Do you hang around with kids who drink?

— — 15. Do most of your friends drink less than you?

YES NO

— — 16. Do you drink until you are drunk or the bottle is empty?

— — 17. Have you ever had a loss of memory from drinking?

— — 18. Have you ever been to a hospital or arrested for drunk driving or being drunk in public or at school?

— — 19. Do you turn off to any studies or lectures about drinking?

— — 20. Do you think you may have a problem with liquor?

— — TOTALS

If you answered "yes" to one question, it could be a warning that you are becoming a problem drinker. If you answered "yes" to two questions, you might already be a problem drinker. If you answered "yes" to three questions, you probably are a problem drinker. Think about who you can approach for help…then do it!

Chapter 11

Learning to Intervene

Both of us host daily radio programs that generate numerous phone calls and emails from people who have a variety of religious convictions. These folks want help because they, or someone they love, have reached a point of crisis. They contact us ready to take action, yet they often fail to act because they hold beliefs that prevent finding a solution. We are amazed how some people use Christianity to avoid taking responsibility.

One day a lady called my (Steve's) program who desperately needed to read Dr. James Dobson's book *Love Must Be Tough*. (She also needed a good dose of common sense.) She believed you could sit back and love anyone into changing. Concerned about her alcoholic husband and drug-using son, she wanted to know how to pray better to bring about change.

The phone counselor recommended she perform an intervention on both her husband and son to motivate them to get help. She was unwilling. "It would show a lack of faith," she said. "It wouldn't be the Christian thing to do." We think she didn't fully understand Christianity.

Parents Need to Show "Tough Love"

The New Testament tells of a gentle and loving Christ who came to a point where He finally had enough and performed the first intervention in recorded history. We know He greatly loved the money changers in the Temple, as He loves all human beings. His love finally brought Him to a point of being unwilling to watch the money changers continue their destructive behaviors. So He overturned their tables and threw them out of the Temple. Very quickly they felt the consequences of their behavior (see Matthew 21:12-13).

Like Christ, we sometimes must make the tough decision to stop someone from moving down a path of destruction. We must intervene. We must love a person so much that we act on his or her behalf, although acting may be painful for that person and for ourselves.

Education Before Intervention

Long before intervention is necessary, parents should teach their children about alcohol and drugs, beginning as early as kindergarten and elementary school. The education should be backed up by training that involves increasing rewards for responsible behavior and increasing restrictions for irresponsible acts. Parents need to know how to identify the use of alcohol and drugs and focus their attention on their kids' appearance, behavior, and peers.

If you detect chemical abuse by your children, the next step is to intervene so the addiction does not progress one day longer than it has to. This chapter will help you understand the intervention process. Because of intervention, thousands of people have been spared their lives, families, careers, and, especially in the case of adolescents, their futures.

Kids in Denial

Once you identify that your child has a drug or alcohol problem, as a responsible parent, you must not only break through your own denial, but also help your child with his or her refusal to see the problem. Keep in mind that your children's denial will be stronger than yours. Whatever your children admit to is probably the tip of the iceberg. Multiply what you know of the problem by five, and you will be closer to the seriousness of the situation.

Once confronted, your children will deny the accusations to protect what they have come to depend on. Do not listen to the minimization and rationalization. The intervention process is a powerful tool that can break through your kids' denial.

Hitting Bottom

Like adults, kids will use drugs and alcohol until they hit bottom. For years, those working with alcoholics and drug addicts believed people had to hit bottom on their own. You would hear statements such as, "That guy has a lot more drinking to do before anyone can help him." The theory was that everyone should sit around and watch an addict lose family, friends, money, job, freedom, and everything else, then he or she would realize that the only way to go is up. Recovery doesn't have to begin under those circumstances.

Sometimes a crisis or a tragedy, especially a life-threatening tragedy, can break the cycle. Some kids stop using drugs or alcohol when they are in an automobile accident and are almost killed or lose a limb. The glimmer of death motivates them to reach out for help.

For others, a drug overdose leaves them just this side of death, and they recover from the drug use intent on never using them again. Seeing a friend die or come close to death is tragedy enough to change the course of drug usage for some kids. But no one should wait for an unforeseen crisis or tragedy to effect change in the life of a child. That has happened too often, resulting in needless handicaps and loss of life.

All the horrible consequences of out-of-control addiction can be avoided through the process of intervention. This process helps people face the reality of the drug or alcohol problem, hit bottom in a controlled environment, and begin recovery. Forcing children to hit bottom early raises their levels of "bottom," enabling them to recover more quickly and have much more of life intact. Intervention nearly always changes the addict for the better, and it always changes the family for good.

The Intervention Process

The intervention process refers to a series of actions taken by the family that will lead to change in the addict. Because most change is brought about by a crisis, intervention precipitates a crisis. It brings the full weight and pain of the addictive behavior onto the person. Just as soothing family pain prevents recovery, so turning up the volume on the pain forces needed changes. In doing these things, a stable-but-miserable situation is disrupted, making room for growth. Here is what an intervention process looks like.

Assessment

When a family decides to intervene with a child, the first step is an assessment of the family by a professional. The assessment is designed to determine several things, including the family's strength. If the family has been living on eggshells for some time and family members are involved in destructive behavior, they may be too weak to be effective with the child. The parents may need counseling to strengthen themselves before they can help in the intervention process.

The other reason for the assessment is to determine whether other members of the family are chemically dependent. Many interventions have been destroyed when the addict pointed out that his or her substance abuse was no worse than that of someone else in the family. Parents need to treat their own chemical dependencies first.

If chemical dependency is not detected among other family members, if they have adequate strength to perform the intervention, and if addiction is verified in the child, the counselor will recommend that the process continue.

Classes

The family must then attend classes to become familiar with addiction, codependency, and intervention. These classes are offered through most drug treatment facilities. Some counselors specialize in the intervention process. You will be able to find classes by placing just a few phone calls.

Family members will be required to attend a lecture on how addiction progresses and follows a predictable path leading either to death, insanity, or recovery. They will be given reading assignments to reinforce that others have also had children trapped in addiction. They learn, too, about the enabling process and how everyone in the family has sheltered the addict from the consequences of his or her behavior.

As the family learns about enabling and other destructive roles, its behavior toward the addict begins to change. That is why many interventions never occur; the addict senses that something is happening and may volunteer for treatment before the event can take place. The final information the family learns is how to conduct an intervention, including how to accumulate data that can be used effectively in the intervention.

Intervention Rehearsal

After the classes are presented, the family members conduct an intervention rehearsal. They go through what they will say as the counselor playacts what the addict is likely to do in reaction. The family practices instructing the addict about which alternatives are acceptable and which are not. For instance, the family determines that maintaining the status quo is not acceptable, and it decides what form of treatment would be best for the child. When the intervention is adequately rehearsed, the family and counselor set a date for the event.

Intervention Data

The data for the intervention are carefully collected to help the addict see the need for help. The data must conform to the following guidelines:

- They must be related to the drinking or drug-taking behavior or to events actually witnessed.
- They must include consumption levels and consequences. For example: "Ted, you drank two bottles of

wine and stuffed them under your bed. That night you got out of bed, fell down the stairs, and broke your wrist."

- They must include the date and time the drinking or drugging occurred.
- They must always be presented with care and concern.
- They must include feelings related to the drinking and drugging events.
- They must point out the contradictions and conflicts in values and behaviors.
- They must acknowledge attempts to control, quit, or change behavior.

When all the data adhere to these guidelines, they are very effective in helping the addict face reality.

Intervention-Offered Alternatives

The family must agree on acceptable and unacceptable alternatives for the addict. The primary alternative is for the addict to seek professional help from a quality treatment center. If the addict refuses professional help, a secondary alternative is spelled out— perhaps going to an Alcoholics Anonymous meeting each week, stopping drinking, and obtaining help from addiction specialists.

Sometimes an addict simply cannot be moved to seek help, and then the "what if" clause must be used. It outlines a predetermined course of action if the drinking or drugging happens again. This would include agreeing to obtain intensive treatment or leaving the house if help continues to be rejected. The family members should also plan alternatives for themselves, such as separation, family therapy, or involvement in a support group. These are not presented as threats but as choices for the long-term good of the family.

The Intervention Event

The event is a therapeutic session in which the addict is confronted with data concerning specific situations, the feelings he or she caused the family members to experience, and what the family wants the addict to do. The entire session is designed to motivate the addicted person to get help. In a typical intervention, the counselor asks the addict to commit to staying in the session for at least one hour. The addict is told that each person in the room is there because he or she cares and wants to discuss some information.

When the commitment is obtained, the session begins. The family members take turns presenting information—the data—while the addict listens. Each person relates two or three events and his or her reactions and feelings. When everyone is done, the alternatives are presented and the addict is asked to get help. If the person does not agree to get help, the contingency plan is enacted, and the addict might be asked to leave home until he or she is willing to seek help. That rarely happens, however, because the person almost always agrees. But whatever the outcome, the addict's behavior will never be the same. The "game" is over because the family has become wise to the progression of the problem and is resolved not to let it continue unchallenged.

Why Intervention Works

After months or years of unsuccessfully trying everything to stop a chemical abuse problem, some people find it hard to believe that intervention produces change in almost every case. But it does produce change, and some clear reasons show why it is so effective.

First, a professional is in charge. The addict is not responding to the emotional strains that exist between family members. The counselor has the most direct interaction with the addict and maintains control over the session. Having a professional in charge makes it unlikely the person will storm out of the room in anger. The professional also prevents the session from becoming a shouting match and keeps everyone focused on the problem and what needs to be done. This stops any attempts to disrupt the process.

During the intervention training process, family members have had a chance to work through some of their anger and resentment resulting from the drug or alcohol abuse. So they come to the intervention with their emotions in check. Their lack of hostility is mirrored by the addict. The person's defensiveness is greatly reduced when he or she senses this is not a yelling, blaming, or condemning session.

Realizing the family's concern helps produce the needed result for the addict. As family members present information to the addict, he or she can't help but hear and sense the support in their voices. Perhaps for the first time in years, the addict hears the family speak without judging or criticizing. That change has a powerful effect—the addict knows something is different and something must change.

Staying "On Topic"

All the information presented is related to out-of-control behavior, so the addict doesn't feel personally attacked. The person hears about recent events, all involving drugs or alcohol, all involving negative consequences, and all causing the family uncomfortable emotions. This has a tremendous influence because no one hints that the person is bad or inadequate. Rather, the problem has been documented and presented in such an objective form that it cannot be denied, and personal attacks have been completely excluded.

Talking to a patient after an intervention had been performed with her, I (Steve) asked how she felt during the process. She told me she experienced initial anger followed by relief. Then she made a most important statement—the intervention was the first time anyone had talked to her in a way she could hear. I believe that is because the intervention process takes away the need to be defensive.

Clearly Defined Goal

The other factor making intervention successful is a clearly defined direction and goal for the session. The child is asked to see the reality of his or her drinking or drugging and then asked to do something about it. Of course, almost everyone in that situation will say, "Okay, I'll stop forever. No, really, I mean it. You convinced me. I'll never touch the stuff again."

But intervention works beyond that because the alternatives have been prearranged. The addict thinks he or she can get off the hook by admitting what the evidence has proved and saying it has changed his or her life. But once the addict makes the admission, the choices of help and treatment are presented. That is when the full force of the intervention takes hold because then each family member declares his or her love and a deep desire that the addict take advantage of the help that has already been arranged. Those tough-loving family members, committed to helping the person recover, produce the first step of hope in the life of the addict.

Intervention—Hard Work but Worth the Effort

Intervention is not easy because addiction to alcohol and drugs is powerful. Intervention is not the ultimate solution, and it never happens exactly according to plan. Nor does the intervention alone cause needed changes in the family. The decision by the parents to intervene is the *beginning* of the change process. And because denial is so strong and recurring, some form of intervention will have to happen again and again. Until the addict has taken full responsibility for his or her actions and recovery, every day can be another small intervention that moves the person toward recovery.

Intervention has helped tens of thousands of addicts. In recent years, country music star Keith Urban, actors Mel Gibson and Joaquin Phoenix, model Kate Moss, and numerous sports greats have sought help. And the vast majority of interventions produce a recovering person who goes on to motivate others toward recovery. Imagine how many people your children may affect after you intervene and lead them toward recovery. Each intervention can save a life; sometimes it can save hundreds of lives.

Chapter 12

Getting Help

Ronnie convinced his parents that the small pouch of cocaine they found in his room was a remnant of a past life. The drugs were there only because he forgot to throw them out. He persuaded them to help him start a new life. All he needed was a car, and he could find work. They agreed to the plan and purchased the car, stipulating that he had to make payments from the money he earned. He turned the agreement into an opportunity for gain through manipulation. For about the hundredth time, his parents had taken the bait.

The tragedy occurred only three days after the new car was first parked in the driveway. First, the assistant principal called from the high school to ask where Ronnie was. A random check had uncovered Ronnie's truancy. But that was just the beginning. The next call came from a police officer, who informed Ronnie's parents that he had been involved in a crash while driving under the influence of alcohol. He had been taken to a hospital and had suffered a concussion. At the hospital, his mother was given the phone number of a treatment center.

By the time I (Steve) saw him, Ronnie was ready to begin a new life, and he did. His parents by his side, he started over again with the help of a treatment team that gave him tools to stay sober. Not everyone uses the tools, but Ronnie did—and still does.

Taking the First Step

If your children have been identified as having alcohol or drug problems, you want the professional help that will benefit them the most. You must fight back the urge to handle the problem alone. Drug addiction and alcoholism are powerful forces. In Proverbs 20:18, the wise person is urged to seek good counsel when waging war. That is what you must do if you are going to win.

This chapter will help you make wise decisions about the kind of help you obtain for your kids. All programs and counselors are not the same. Some have very different values and beliefs from yours. Knowing that, many parents make no decision because they are afraid of throwing their children to the wolves. Their fears are valid, but their actions are not. The guidelines presented here will enable you to find help by having the confidence that your children will be strengthened and your values will be supported.

When Does a Person Need Professional Help?

Most people seek professional help much later than they should. They wish for the best or think problems will get better—after the holidays, when work pressure subsides, or after graduation. Unfortunately, in drug and alcohol abuse, things usually get worse before they get better.

The natural tendency is to try to handle all our problems ourselves, including our children's chemical abuse. But if everything you have tried has failed, it is time to get help. Seeking help is not a sign of weakness; it's a sign of strength and love.

Some people advocate doing as little as possible for as long as possible. But this can cause failure or, at the least, wasted time. You need to put every force available to work on the problem, treating it as a spreading cancer that must be cut out immediately. Any extra time and money will be well spent if it produces the recovery you desire. Are you willing to do whatever it takes to help your child recover? To go the extra mile rather then choose what appears to be the easiest path?

Why It's Important to Get Help

Chemical abuse affects every area of a person's life. The mind doesn't work properly because it has been saturated with chemicals. The body is chemically imbalanced. And the soul of a person, along with values and beliefs, is damaged. For an addict to recover, each area must be treated. That is why professional care is needed. No one person can treat the totality of a person experiencing the severe problems associated with drug addiction or alcoholism.

Some addicts have recovered on their own by attending a support group. But many have also walked away after one meeting and thought it was not for them. Some addicts have prayed, been immediately delivered from their addiction, and gone for years without a drink or a drug. Others have made an instantaneous, miraculous recovery, only to start drinking or using again a few months later. And many more have been praying for years and have not changed at all.

It's easy to focus on the quickest and most convenient method. It is especially easy if that appears to be the more spiritual approach. But too many failures have occurred for any single approach to be used for this complex problem. Obtaining professional help brings together a variety of disciplines to help you help your children win the battle.

When to Bring in a Professional

The need for professional help is obvious in some cases, such as when medical attention is required. An addicted person going through withdrawal from drugs is an example. This is something a pastor or other counselor cannot treat alone. In extreme cases, it is possible for a person to suffer physical or neurological brain damage if a naive counselor does not seek medical advice. The medical profession is equipped to handle these life-threatening problems. When help is sought, it is important to obtain it from a resource that is intent on helping without destroying the supports already in place for the addict.

How to Find Quality Help

Any quality helping professional or organization, whether a church, community resource program, or therapist, should know the best resources available. But sometimes these organizations have not done the research yet, which means you will have to do more on your own. When you start your search for helpers, don't ask only about drug and alcohol addiction. Treatment should be holistic and include a positive approach to morals, family, and Christian beliefs. A well-balanced program focuses not only on the addiction, but also takes into consideration the spiritual, mental, physical, and social aspects of life.

When a young person is clearly diagnosed as having an addiction, we are partial to a program that uses a treatment *team* rather than a single counselor or pastor. For example, when a young person is admitted to an inpatient program or outpatient clinic, a team of qualified and caring therapists, doctors, nurses, and other professionals combine their strengths to overpower the grip of addiction. Any one of these professionals acting separately would be unable to devote the time and energy usually needed to address addiction problems. The staff must be willing to do whatever is required. But so must the patient. When patient, family, and treatment team are all willing to do whatever it takes for as long as necessary, the hope for change is tremendous.

A Case Study in Denial

While working in treatment in California, we saw many affluent parents who were unwilling to admit they couldn't help their children who had alcohol and drug problems. They could manage large companies and major charities, so they thought they should be able to handle any problem that arose within the family. But parents from all walks of life struggle with asking for help. It's hard for parents to give up control and allow someone else to assist. But parents must reach that point if their children are to be given the best chance to recover.

When does a person need professional help? Usually *now*. If you have been asking that question, it is time to stop questioning and start acting.

Rebuilding Lives

In every life, certain key moments usher in change and hope for a new beginning. Those moments are rare, however, so if someone in your family has come to the point of realizing the need for change and desires help, it is important that good decisions be made the first time around. It could be some time, or maybe never, before the opportunity or motivation to change will come again. You don't want to waste what could be the best chance for change.

Also, few people have unlimited resources to pay for treatment. Whether paying all the costs or just the deductible portion after insurance, your money should go toward the greatest hope for help. Most people rely on insurance to cover the bulk of the expense, but many insurance companies limit the amount they will pay or the days they will cover a person in treatment. Those precious dollars must not be wasted on ineffective or inappropriate treatment.

More important than money or resources, of course, is the need for the person you love to be in a program that is constructive rather than destructive. Programs vary in their effectiveness, and some can do more harm than good. In some treatment centers, for example, poor supervision allows drug dealers and other patients to bring in drugs. This kind of environment clearly is not good and can destroy any possibility for recovery.

In some programs, the problem can be drugs from a source other than drug dealers. For instance, some programs overutilize medication to control patients. This, combined with an unstructured program, can be a miserable experience for those being treated. They can become further trapped in their problems. Medication is not bad for all patients; sometimes, although rarely, it is a necessity. But if it is used too frequently or liberally, the effect can be to move patients from one addiction to another.

Some programs have other counterproductive elements. Probably the most prevalent and the most serious are destructive attitudes and behaviors. When you go to a treatment center, for example, you might sense a mood of depression or high anxiety from both staff and patients. If a visitor can sense this mood in a short time, you can imagine how strong those feelings must be for the patients who are there 24 hours a day. The negative environment is created by unhealthful staff attitudes and behaviors, which are always reflected in the patients they treat. It is essential that a person seeking help for the first time find it in a safe and healthful environment where staff are motivated to provide quality care.

Types of Programs

Many types of treatment programs are available. Each has its strengths and its weaknesses. We have tried to list each type, along with a few comments. At the end of chapter 16, we have provided a national resource phone number managed by New Life Clinics. When you call, the counselor can direct you to a local helping agency and help you determine the best type of treatment for your child and your situation.

Inpatient Hospital

Inpatient treatment is conducted in a hospital that has a full complement of medical staff, including doctors and nurses. They are assisted by a team of professionals who have training in social work, psychology, and counseling. This is the most comprehensive treatment available and keeps the patient in a protected environment during the initial phases. This kind of treatment is covered by most major insurance companies.

Residential Treatment

Residential treatment is conducted outside a hospital and is much less expensive than inpatient care. Sometimes it is not covered by insurance. A person requiring medical attention would not do well in this setting. But someone who does not have a medical crisis could find residential treatment an excellent alternative. The medical team is not as strong, although the program staff is usually skilled and experienced. Residential treatment also provides a protected environment and a time away from the family so that healthful adjustments can be made in family relationships.

Halfway House

A halfway house also provides a place for separation from the family, and to a lesser degree than the first two alternatives, provides a protected environment. Everyone in the house is recovering, and most residents attend school or work during the day. When they come back in the evening, residents attend counseling sessions and Alcoholics and Narcotics Anonymous meetings. For those who have had repeated relapses, this is an excellent option for long-term sobriety.

Day Treatment

A strong day-treatment program includes everything found in an inpatient treatment center, except the patients go home at night. This is much less costly than inpatient care, but insurance is just beginning to cover some of these programs in a few locations. When separation from the home is required or a person cannot control the urge to use drugs or alcohol in the initial recovery states, this would not be a good choice.

Outpatient Care

For some, outpatient care is all that is needed. The person goes to a group meeting in the evening after school or work. These programs must be highly structured to be successful, especially with kids who are not yet committed to recovery. Because the hours are fewer and the program less intensive, recovery can be a much more frustrating experience for the family if a relapse occurs. When a relapse does occur, inpatient treatment should be pursued.

Excellent outpatient help, however, can be obtained through local Alcoholics Anonymous and Alateen chapters, group therapy, or private counseling. We are also encouraging churches and youth groups to start small and intensive outpatient groups for kids who have drug and alcohol problems.

Wrong Reasons for Choosing a Treatment Program

In the search for quality treatment, people are motivated by a variety of events and pressures. At times, choosing a program becomes less than a totally objective decision. It is essential that you not make a selection based on wrong reasons. The following are some common reasons for *not* choosing a treatment program.

Newness of Facility

Whenever a new facility opens, public relations announcements and advertising herald the event, and it is easy to get caught up in the hype. The new program may be of the highest possible quality, but you won't know that from press releases and ads. Take the time to find other reasons to choose a program. Remember, the new kid on the block isn't necessarily the best kid.

Extracurricular Activities and Amenities

Some programs take patients horseback riding. They may have a swimming pool on the grounds. The staff may give patients the opportunity to play golf. But these things don't make people well; they merely make the people's stay a little more comfortable. Often people need to feel discomfort before they become or stay motivated to change. If they are made too comfortable or allowed too many diversions from dealing with their problems, treatment can become a waste of time. What creates a great program is the content, the schedule, the quality of groups, and most importantly, the competence of the staff.

Advertising

The thousands of advertisements on television and in newspapers and magazines help motivate people to go into treatment. But a treatment center should not be chosen based on an ad. Commercials are no indication of the level of care available, and many of the best treatment centers do little or no advertising.

The Choice of the Adolescent

When a child is in need of treatment, it is better to rely on your own judgment rather than the desires of the adolescent. An addict has little ability to make a rational decision about the best kind of care needed. What kids do know is which treatment centers have a free flow of drugs. They also know where the drug culture, hard rock and rap, and paraphernalia is allowed and where it is discouraged. Sometimes a child will want to go into a center because a girlfriend or boyfriend is there. But the last person you want choosing the treatment center is the one needing help.

A Physician's Reputation

A parent might see a well-respected doctor on television or hear the doctor on the radio. Because of the doctor's charisma or reputation, the parent might think the treatment program the physician is associated with must be good. But that is not necessarily true. Less than five percent of a patient's time will be spent with a physician. Treatment programs are designed so that the physician is not the only person treating the patient. A team approach is used in many centers, and the team is much more important than any one member, including the physician.

Cost

Drug and alcohol problems are life-and-death matters. Cost should have little to do with where help is obtained. Oftentimes inexpensive programs do not have enough staff to meet patients' needs. Salaries may be so low that only entry-level people are used in the treatment process. It is much better to find the best treatment resource available, and then find a way to finance the cost.

Proximity

If all else were equal, the closer the unit, the better the opportunity would be for the entire family to receive treatment. And the more treatment the whole family receives, the greater the chance for total recovery. But fine programs make allowances for out-of-town families. Special tracks are designed to accommodate and treat the whole family so that distance is not as major a factor in recovery. Don't make convenience the biggest part of your decision.

Community Image of the Hospital

A hospital may have a strong reputation that covers up a weak alcohol and drug treatment program. The image of a hospital or the amount of its community service involvement should not be used to measure a treatment program. The drug treatment unit is only a portion of the hospital, and all that matters is what the performance level is in that unit. Horrible acute-care hospitals can have wonderful drug and alcohol units because the two services are often managed by separate organizations.

Correct Reasons for Choosing a Treatment Center

The following reasons are the best ones for choosing a treatment center and offer the greatest hope for obtaining effective help.

A Well-Maintained Facility

The first indication of a commitment to quality care is a facility that is clean and well-maintained. It doesn't have to be the newest or the biggest or the nicest hospital. But your confidence in the program should be strengthened by the outside appearance and interior maintenance. If the facility is not clean and appears rundown, it is obvious the patients' comfort is not a high priority. But where you find a commitment to the structure of a building, you often find quality care.

A Referral from Someone You Trust

Having so many resources from which to choose, it is always

better to have a recommendation from someone you can trust, someone who has helped many people get help. Your pastor could be an excellent source of guidance if he or she has referred others and is pleased with the results of a particular program. Find several people who have had success, and ask how they did it.

A Referral by a Former Addict

Nothing speaks louder than the successful treatment of a person and his or her long-term recovery. No one knows a program better than someone who has been treated there. If you don't know someone who has been through a program, you might ask the center for the names of successful alumni you can contact. This can help you determine whether the qualities of the program are likely to meet the needs of your family.

A Strong Team Approach

Two basic kinds of programs are available in alcohol and drug treatment:

- *Weak staff, dominant physician.* In these programs, the doctor makes all the decisions about patient care. The rest of the staff, who spend most of the time with the patient, are disregarded in planning the course of treatment. There have been times when a physician has recommended a pass for a patient, and other staff members knew the patient was suicidal. The resulting death could have been avoided if the physician had consulted the staff. A doctor who has a strong ego and disregard for the opinions of other treatment staff can be a detriment to patient care.

- *Strong staff, physician as team member.* In this environment, the nurses, therapists, patient, technicians, and doctor work together to form a treatment plan that covers all the patient's needs. All staff members express their views about the patient before the treatment plan is developed. This is extremely important because most programs have more than one physician involved in the treatment process.

Where a weak staff and a bullying physician team up, the treatment is poor, the care inconsistent, and the results less than satisfactory. Where a strong staff places high value on the effectiveness of the team, a greater chance for quality care occurs. And where this occurs, the staff is more satisfied with their jobs, and the teams stay together longer, providing consistent care over the years.

Healthful Support for a Sober Lifestyle
This includes:

- *Music.* Most programs allow patients to bring in CD and MP3 players and listen to any kind of music they desire. Yet many authorities are now saying heavy metal, hard rock, and rap are not conducive to recovery. This music is full of references to drugs, death, rebellion, immoral sex, and other unhealthful behaviors. This music is an integral part of the drug culture and reinforces the patient's desire to use drugs or alcohol again. A treatment center that controls the patients' music creates a healthier environment for them.

- *Movies.* Viewing movies that focus on violence, sex, and crude language is allowed in many drug treatment units. This also is counterproductive to total lifestyle change. Filling the mind with examples of negative behavior does nothing but reinforce these forms of behavior. Quality care means monitoring what is viewed and providing positive alternatives.

- *Language.* One of the clearest indicators of a person's inner state of mind is reflected in the words he or she chooses to use. Foul language should be discouraged. Good communication that is inoffensive to others helps a person fit into a civil and moral lifestyle.

- *View of sex.* If staff members believe in the personal dignity of the person, they will confront any behavior that is dishonorable or could cause another person to be degraded. Often kids will replace their dependency on drugs with a dependency on sexual pleasure. This behavior must be confronted as soon as it surfaces.

Personal Attention

Poor programs will reveal that individual sessions are not important for quality care. This is because the program has such low staff-to-patient ratios that the staff does not have enough time for individual sessions. To determine whether the people in a program really care, you must find out if they offer individual therapy for all the patients on an almost-daily basis. If the staff-to-patient ratio is low, the quality of care will be low.

Family Treatment

When one person becomes sick with an alcohol or drug problem, the entire family also gets sick. People do not deteriorate in a vacuum. It is important that each person in the family receives help if the patient is to be helped long term. A healthy patient going back into an unhealthy family will become unhealthy again.

We have often seen the person in treatment become the healthiest member of the family. As a sacrificial lamb, that person has allowed him- or herself to be treated so that the whole family will get help. One young girl simply would not go home to her parents. She would relapse just before discharge, and treatment would begin again. Finally someone broke through to what was really happening in her life. She was a victim of sexual abuse, and she didn't want to face those times without drugs. She knew the pain of abuse would lead her back to the chemicals. Her family had not been forced to participate in treatment, so this had not been detected before. For her to return to that dysfunctional family would have been futile. Her family needed treatment as badly as she did.

Staff Attitudes of Sensitivity and Service

Any time a person enters treatment, pain, emotional turmoil, hours of preparation, and money have been expended. The family should expect a lot from the program. The staff should realize what the people have been through to arrive at the need for treatment. Each person—especially the patient—should be approached with great sensitivity. Staff members should display an attitude of service in each encounter with the family.

Traditional Values Supported

When you or someone in your family goes into treatment, you should be assured that traditional values will not be undermined. Religious values should not be challenged, but instead be incorporated into the treatment process. Don't be afraid to ask about staff attitudes toward beliefs you and your family hold dear. If the program cannot support these beliefs, treatment could be counterproductive.

In particular, Christian parents should select a quality Christian program. Many centers talk of a spiritual dimension to treatment, but "spiritual" and "Christian" can be two entirely different things. Some programs, for example, take their patients to the desert for an experience that combines Indian folklore, astrology, and pantheism. Such an experience would be a Christian parent's nightmare. And because recovering addicts are at a point of change and strongly desire to learn a new way of life, they are impressionable and easily led astray. Prevent your children from focusing on the power of man or the gods of nonbelievers by seeking the best treatment in a Christian setting delivered by Christian professionals.

Components of Quality Care

It is difficult to describe what constitutes quality treatment. You can't just compile a list and say that if the items on the list are present, quality care is guaranteed. It is more complicated than that. Quality care is a *process* that occurs over time; it has many people interacting and bringing their resources to bear on the patient. Some programs are stronger in certain areas than others. Two programs could use radically different approaches and still provide quality treatment. But to assist you in finding quality care for someone in your family, common components can be identified:

- As mentioned before, the treatment facility does not have to be fancy or new, but it should be clean and well-maintained. Never leave a person at a facility of which you cannot be proud.

- The overall attitude of the staff must show love and concern. Harsh, angry staff produce harsh, angry patients. However don't confuse tough love with bad attitude.

- The staff should have plenty of experience and excellent credentials. Low-paid, underqualified, and inexperienced staff cannot provide quality treatment.

- A strong team approach should be used because it means a patient will get the most appropriate care. Often a patient can fool one or two staff members or remain in denial if few people give input into treatment. But when a team is at work, the patient is more likely to deal with reality.

- Visitors should be monitored closely. Treatment is a time to focus on change, not old friends. Often those who come to visit are people with whom the patient should not associate.

- Television, music, reading material, dress, language, and attitude should all be supervised by the staff so that each patient contributes to a positive environment, allowing everyone the greatest chance to change.

- The treatment provided should be a blend of group, individual, and family therapy. Lectures, films, and discussion groups should fill a patient's day. Little time should be available to sit and do nothing.

- Family treatment must also be a priority. Putting a recovering patient back into a sick family makes relapse likely.

- Never commit someone in your family to a program

that will undermine the spiritual foundation you have
established.

- Quality treatment addresses the whole person. The
physical, mental, emotional, social, and spiritual areas
must all be considered.

- The program should include attendance at some kind
of follow-up support group. This ongoing aftercare is
the best insurance that all areas will continue to be
addressed.

- Whatever the cost, quality care must be the priority.
Where quality care is given, patients get well. As mentioned before, the best indicator of a program's quality
is in observing what has happened in the lives of those
who received treatment.

Treatment is a great opportunity for an entire family to recover.
If your children need help, do not delay in seeking professional
assistance.

Chapter 13

Parents' Guide to Handling Relapse

For three years the McMillans tried to help their son. They took him out of one school and put him in another. They promised him a car and money for college. They pleaded and cajoled, but the situation grew worse each day. Finally they realized that only treatment could help their boy. His drug problem would not respond to home remedies.

They consulted the Yellow Pages, looked under "Alcohol and Drug Treatment Centers," and made the call. For the first time in three years, they felt hope. The counselor guided them through the process of intervention, resulting in their son going into treatment.

The boy did well in the program. The therapists loved him and enjoyed having him in their groups. He was a leader among the other kids. He told everyone he really wanted to make a new start. And while at the center, he wrote letters to all his drug-using friends, telling them of his new, sober life. As he showed the letters to his parents, their hopes soared. The son they loved was theirs to enjoy again.

Three weeks after graduation from the program, the boy was arrested for possession of methamphetamines. As the McMillans drove to the police station, the word "failure" summed up all their thoughts and emotions. They thought their son had failed. They thought they had failed. And they thought the treatment center had failed.

Relapse Remorse

The McMillans' reaction was typical for the common post-treatment event called "relapse." But "relapse" and "failure" *are not* synonymous. For most people in recovery, relapse becomes the first stage of true progress based on reality, not false expectations. This proved to be true for the McMillans. Their son's relapse was not the end of recovery, but the real beginning. It forced him to see the need for a *comprehensive* recovery plan that went far *beyond* determination and motivation.

Relapse Is Common

People hope treatment is a quick, once-and-for-all fix that will result in no more struggles for the family. But treatment is the *beginning* of the fix, not the fix itself. At least 40 percent of those who obtain help will relapse within the first year. Relapse fully acquaints addicts with the reality of their situations. If your children have obtained treatment, you must be prepared for relapses.

When we first began working with alcoholics and drug addicts, we were intensely saddened whenever we heard of a relapse. We viewed each one as a failure. Then we saw wonderful things happen as a result of relapse. Real recovery often began on the other side. Families pulled together in ways they should have when treatment ended.

Once a relapse occurs, the patient and family often develop a workable recovery plan. Treatment does not end when a person graduates from a program or is discharged from a hospital. Such formal treatment only forms the foundation of a recovery process that should continue for the rest of the addict's life. Although the treatment experience may have been negative or the foundation was not as strong as it could have been, recovery can be successful if the family supports a plan of honoring sobriety. Of all the things that happen in a treatment program, the best is that the child and family leave with a recovery plan.

Preparing for the Probable

Good coaches prepare a team for the struggle ahead. They practice game-like situations so team members will be fully prepared. And good coaches develop a plan they will follow during the competition. But the best coaches always go a step further. They also prepare the team for setbacks so the players know what to do if the other team scores first. The team does not suffer a total shock, and a new part of the game plan is implemented.

This is what a good recovery plan should do too. It not only prepares the recovering addict to succeed, but it also charts the steps to pursue if relapse occurs. What is a good recovery plan, and how is it used in preventing relapse or bringing good out of relapse?

Recovery and Relapse Protection Plan

A comprehensive plan for recovery will address every area of a person's life. The longer the recovery is maintained, the more the plan will improve the quality of life. One of the most often-heard mistakes is that a recovery plan neglected one or more areas in the treatment plan. This is why a well-balanced, holistic plan is a must. The following is a list of the most important guidelines for each area of the recovery plan.

Physical

Recovering people tend to neglect the body and its special needs, and this makes recovery much more difficult. Three areas need to be addressed:

1. *Nutrition.* The body pays a heavy price for addiction. The tissues and organs are damaged by the toxicity of the drugs and the poor nutrition that accompanies addiction. Eating habits need to change to ensure that the body can recover strength and rebuild

damaged tissue. Without a balanced diet, the body will limp along. In addition, most recovery professionals recommend vitamin and mineral supplements.

Nutrition is also important to help stabilize blood-sugar levels. When these levels are increased through food and drinks high in sugar, the subsequent drop in blood sugar causes a strong sense of craving, restlessness, and often depression. Stories abound of people who began binge eating on sugary foods, such as ice cream, and relapse within days.

Emotional Eating Can Trigger Relapse

I (Jim) know of a 22-year-old who had been sober for two years. She had just broken up with her fiancé. Her relapse did not begin with a binge of drinking but with a binge of eating. She started consuming food high in sugar. At a party for her niece, she was out of control, eating several helpings of cake and ice cream. Five hours later, when the sugar high wore off, she found alcohol and began drinking again.

The best diet is high in protein, such as fish and poultry, and complex carbohydrates found in fresh vegetables, pasta, and other foods made from grains. Protein-rich foods and fresh vegetables are the best diet to reduce blood-sugar variances. It also helps to eat smaller meals more frequently rather than three large meals a day, which causes the blood-sugar levels to surge and recede dramatically.

Non-Alcoholic Beverage Alert

Many recovering people are able to adjust their food intake, but they fail in the area of beverages. They either load up on highly sugared soft drinks containing plenty of caffeine, or they consume hundreds of cups of coffee filled with caffeine. In kids, of course, the soft-drink binge becomes the biggest sugar and caffeine problem. Both sugar and caffeine produce a stimulating or hyper effect, but it doesn't last. As the blood-sugar level drops, the sensation of craving reaches a peak. This can lead to a relapse as the craving becomes uncontrollable.

Regulating caffeine and sugar intake also strengthens the recovery process by keeping the addict from experiencing extreme emotional highs and lows. Besides, recovery means learning to live without chemicals of any kind—clean and sober. For years, alcoholics have recovered while smoking and drinking coffee. But today we better understand the harmful effects of nicotine and caffeine. Thus, the decision to avoid nicotine and caffeine is a quality issue—the purer the recovery, the higher the quality of recovery.

2. *Exercise.* Exercise offers tremendous recovery benefits. It is the most natural form of stimulation and relaxation, building up strength and stamina while burning off stress. It is a productive way to fill time and work off boredom rather than allow boredom to lead to relapse. It also provides a sense of accomplishment, builds self-esteem, and increases body tone while decreasing body fat. Exercise can help bring a family back together too. Running, jogging, tennis, volleyball, bicycling, swimming, and skiing all provide fun times for the family to mend. People in recovery often feel like a time bomb, ready to explode at any minute. Exercise is the best way to defuse that bomb.

3. *Rest and relaxation.* In addition to proper nutrition and exercise, the body needs plenty of rest, especially in the early stages of recovery. An adolescent coming out of treatment is used to going to bed at 10:00 or 11:00. This schedule should be maintained. A proper amount of rest prevents depression and irritability and eliminates extended periods of temptation. The sleep pattern should vary little, including weekends.

Another helpful tool is for the addict to take scheduled breaks for relaxation. Stopping to refocus in the middle of a hectic schedule can prevent the stress buildup that could trigger a relapse. The wise addict learns to recognize the extreme pressure situations and control them before they become so intense they cannot be controlled. Knowing when to leave a situation and find a quiet corner in a hall or a restroom helps keep the body relaxed and the emotions steady.

Mental

What a person thinks forms the basis for many feelings. If a person is always thinking about the horrible realities of life instead of the wonderful possibilities, it is only natural to be depressed. A strong relapse protection plan exposes the addict to people and events that provide positive material for growth and understanding. The apostle Paul put it this way: "Finally, brothers, whatever is true, whatever is noble, whatever is right, whatever is pure, whatever is lovely, whatever is admirable—if anything is excellent or praiseworthy—think about such things" (Philippians 4:8).

Every recovery plan for adolescents should include reading material on addiction and recovery designed especially for kids. This will help the adolescents stay focused on the successful recoveries of others and the guidelines leading to long-term sobriety. In the recovering community, hundreds of tapes are filled with stories of success. Acquire these tapes, and during tough times, review the ones that are most helpful.

Creating a Community of Support

The key to focusing the mind in a positive manner is attending live lectures and meetings such as Alcoholics Anonymous or Narcotics Anonymous. Coming face-to-face with fellow strugglers in a large group helps to keep the thought process on track. Hearing other people's recovery stories, full of struggle and hopes, adds new insights. It also prevents isolation. Be sure your children are scheduled to hear some good speakers and lectures. Also, find seminars you can attend together.

Addicts need to experience new and powerful information about recovery. This is different from therapy, where emotions are shared and processed. If a child leaves treatment and only attends group therapy, the mental part of recovery will be neglected. So much negative input occurs at school and after school that life becomes discouraging. It is easy for a teenager's thinking to become confused about drugs and recovery. If you don't plan to counter those negative messages, their powerful influence could subvert the entire recovery process. So guide addicts to places where healthy thinking can be reinforced.

We Are What We Think

We tell kids the age-old adage, "Garbage in, garbage out." If they put garbage into their minds, garbage will come out. If they put good thoughts into their minds, good thoughts will come out.

A young man went to a psychologist for help. He was experiencing the same dream every night. He told the counselor, "Every night a black cat and a white cat fight until one of them wins."

The psychologist asked, "Which one wins, the white one or the black one?"

The young man replied, "Whichever one I feed the most."

We must teach young people that what they put into their minds will play a major role in how well they recover. We challenge young people to consider reading through the New Testament or the entire Bible in one year. It is incredible what the wisdom of the Bible can do. "For, 'All men are like grass, and all their glory is like the flowers of the field; the grass withers and the flowers fall, but the word of the Lord stands forever'" (1 Peter 1:24-25).

Emotional

Getting the proper nutrition, exercise, and mental input gives the emotions a greater chance of being steady and strong, able to avoid the dangerous extremes that trigger relapse. But emotional health also requires group sessions where feelings can be explored and expressed. Emotional recovery does not happen in isolation. Recovering adolescents must stay connected to others who are recovering and share with them their emotional ups and downs.

Recovering people often say they stopped growing up when they started drinking or using drugs. Many of these people at age 30 or 40 emotionally still feel like children. Give your kids experiences at home and in groups of recovering people where feelings can be identified, expressed, and managed. The goal is to help them mature into people who can handle emotional trauma without turning back to alcohol or drugs.

Social

As we have emphasized elsewhere, the social pressures on adolescents are extremely strong and difficult to counter. Alcoholics Anonymous talks about "changing playmates and playgrounds." For the alcoholic to recover, his or her choice of friends and hangouts must change. This is especially true for adolescents. As mentioned earlier, the clearest indicator that your children use drugs is that they have friends who are known drug users. The clearest indicator of relapse is that your kids are associating with known drinkers and drug abusers.

Bad Company Corrupts Good Character

Past drug-using friends must be replaced with "clean kids," and whenever possible, with church groups. Your children hanging on to past acquaintances is evidence that treatment did little to adjust their lifestyles. If this is the case, you may have to limit access to certain friends. Total restriction from a person is rarely helpful; it makes the attraction stronger in many instances. But you don't have to allow your children to be out with someone until 3:00 in the morning or be with that person every night of the week. When children cannot control themselves, you must assume more control.

One of the best ways to counter negative social experiences is to provide positive alternatives as a family. Encourage your children to invite other kids to your house for dinner. Plan weekend trips to the lake or beach and invite your children's friends to come along. If a concert is coming to town, plan to take your children with their friends. Be creative, and teach your children to create situations that will be supportive of a sober lifestyle.

Spiritual

Recovery is first and foremost a spiritual process. It is a journey out of the pleasures of the physical world and into the joys of spiritual life. Yet few people understand the importance of spiritual growth as a vital element of recovery.

Any person coming into recovery brings the weight of responsibility for a damaged past and guilt about the pain he or she has caused others. In spiritual recovery, the guilt, shame, and remorse are resolved. If they are not resolved, it will be only a short time before the pain of guilt wears away the resistance to drink and take drugs. The recovery process will be shallow, a form of coping rather than a way to live abundantly and full of God's love. Each successful recovery, on the other hand, is established by having a full understanding of a loving and forgiving God whose Son paid the price for our guilt.

Strength for Today, Hope for Tomorrow

Spiritual recovery is not just for resolving the past, however. It also helps people find a purpose in life beyond material gain or recognition by others. Spiritual growth leads them to discover a life's mission beyond vocation.

Just because someone acknowledges God does not mean the person has achieved spiritual recovery. It is more comprehensive than that. To grow spiritually, each day must be turned over to and be directed by God. Knowledge of Him needs to develop through worship, fellowship, Bible study, and prayer. Without these ingredients, spiritual growth is weak. We believe the "higher power" referred to in the 12-step programs is not some obscure concept, but the God of the Bible, and people can actually have a relationship with their "higher power" through Jesus Christ.

As a parent, you can set the pattern for spiritual growth. Through your own prayer life, Bible study, and church attendance, you lead the way. Don't expect your children to grow spiritually if you are not in the process of growing. If you want to see a miraculous transformation in your children, lead the way down the path of spiritual recovery.

Sample Recovery and Relapse Protection Plan

Before an addict graduates from treatment, it is essential that a recovery and relapse prevention plan be developed. It should address each of the five dimensions just discussed. It should also have a contingency plan to follow if and when the original plan is abandoned or relapse occurs. The following is an example of what a recovery plan could look like.

Relapse Protection and Recovery Plan

To have a full and meaningful recovery, I will do the following things to help maintain my sobriety one day at a time. Jesus said, "Live one day at a time" (Matthew 6:34 TLB).

Physical

1. Jog 20 minutes each afternoon after school.
2. Stay away from soft drinks and desserts, except for desserts after special meals.
3. Take two breaks each day when stress builds up.
4. Eat chicken, fish, beef, or another source of protein. Also consume fresh vegetables every day, along with a vitamin and mineral supplement.

Mental

1. Attend one lecture on recovery at a treatment center each month.
2. Listen to at least one tape on recovery each week. Write a paragraph about one important point from it.
3. Attend at least one speaker-meeting a week.
4. Read a passage from *The Big Book of Alcoholics Anonymous* and some other book about recovery every day.
5. Read the Bible daily.

Emotional

1. Attend at least two discussion groups a week.
2. Continue to see a counselor until anger is worked out.
3. Write in a journal each day about struggles and new challenges.
4. Attend one aftercare group a week.

Social

1. Create a list of people who are negative influences and commit to spending little time with them.
2. Create a list of people who are healthy influences and commit to spending a lot of time with them.
3. Go on at least one family outing a month that I plan.
4. Participate in church group activities.

Spiritual

1. Read the Bible every day.
2. Pray each day that God will use me and help me find a mission in life.
3. Attend church each Sunday I am in town and not sick.
4. Listen to at least one tape a month on spiritual recovery.

The following will take place if I fail to follow the recovery plan

1. Phone my counselor for treatment and set up an appointment to discuss any problems or discouragements I might be having.
2. If this talk does not change my behavior and attitude, I will return to treatment before I use drugs or alcohol again. Treatment may be in the form of seeing an addiction specialist, attending an outpatient program, or going into a hospital.
3. If I am picked up by the police for an alcohol- or drug-related offense, my parents will assume I am guilty and not bail me out of jail or spend money for me to plead innocent. I

understand they will allow me to experience the full weight
of the consequences of my behavior.

_____

Signed

_____

Date

Planning the Work, Working the Plan

I (Steve) once worked with a beautiful young girl on her plan
for recovery. Nothing in the plan was left uncovered. She was ready
for a new life. But we had just one problem. She went home and
put her plan in a drawer and never looked at it again. Her parents
also neglected to hold her accountable. She relapsed and was full of
guilt and shame when she returned to treatment. If your children
obtain treatment and develop recovery plans, be sure to hold them
accountable. It is one of the best assurances for a strong recovery.

Relapse Indicators

The first indicator of relapse is not your child becoming stoned
or drunk again. Other signs and symptoms are expressed long before
then. If you see these signs, you can intervene at the beginning of
the relapse progression, before the total relapse occurs.

The relapse progression starts with complacency. People in
relapse stop doing all the things that help maintain sobriety, and
then they become confused. Without wholesome influence, they
begin to wonder just how bad the problem really was, doubting
they were truly addicted. Next they begin to compromise, going to
the wrong places and setting themselves up for failure. Then finally
the catastrophe occurs. They return to drinking and drugging. The
entire recovery process is stopped, and everyone must begin again.

These four stages of relapse are a predictable progression as easily
recognized as the initial progression toward addiction. At any point
the progression can stop by using the proper intervention. All a

parent must do is recognize that recovery has been sidetracked and relapse is in the making.

10 Indicators a Young Addict Is Moving from Recovery to Relapse

1. *Negative relationships.* The child begins dating or hanging around with kids known for their heavy drinking and drug taking. This will probably be rationalized as an attempt to help these kids, but it is just a cover-up for the desire to return to negative behavior.

2. *Dishonesty.* He or she starts to lie and is caught in those lies. Lies about insignificant things are a warning that your child is being dishonest in other areas, such as chemical abuse.

3. *A critical spirit.* Your child begins to move away from gratitude and into repeated criticism. This process of projection is often a way of coping with the guilt from irresponsible behavior. Confront the critical comments as soon as you notice them.

4. *Self-centeredness.* This coincides with the critical and ungrateful attitude. When selfishness is evidenced, spiritual and emotional recovery have been hampered.

5. *Isolation.* He or she begins to separate from the family and becomes unwilling to participate in family activities.

6. *Low frustration tolerance.* The child appears to be less able to cope with the minor irritations of life, becoming easily frustrated.

7. *Anxiety.* He or she grows more anxious. Serenity disappears.

8. *Defiance.* Rebellious rage begins to replace love and acceptance.

9. *Grandiosity.* This closely parallels dishonesty. The addict starts to have unrealistic plans, and his conversations are quite removed from reality.

10. *Depression.* He or she is depressed and constantly in a bad mood, spending many hours sleeping.

When these signals begin to surface, your child has become complacent in the recovery plan. The sooner you intervene, the greater the chance to avoid the agony of a relapse.

Ten Threats to Recovery

Knowing the symptoms of relapse doesn't mean you should sit back and wait for them to appear. Instead, work together with your child to identify and avoid the main threats to recovery. These threats are the things that usually trip up recovering people. Learn about them, and discuss them with your kid. And when you see your child succumbing to one or more, warn him or her and help your loved one stay on course. The 10 threats are:

1. *Guilt.* Irresponsible behavior such as dishonesty will produce guilt. Many people drink and abuse drugs in response to unresolved guilt. Responsible behavior is the best way to avoid the problem.

2. *Unhealthy relationships.* Kids don't stay sober with drunk friends.

3. *Holidays.* Reality rarely matches our high expectations of the holidays. Tension is often created in bringing multiple generations together. Parties and advertisements also encourage drinking. These are tough times, and everyone needs to give extra support to recovering addicts.

4. *Hunger.* Blood-sugar levels drop and emotions are on edge in the wake of hunger. A person in recovery should not go too long without eating.

5. *High-pressure situations.* The anticipation of high-pressure situations and the letdown when they have ended send anxiety levels soaring. Before or after these kinds of situations, a recovering person must be aware that feelings are often out of control. He or she needs to learn to wait for anxiety to level off rather than act on impulse to relieve the tension through chemicals. Remember, situations don't have to be negative to produce tension.

6. *Anger.* When resentment builds into anger, danger is at

hand. Millions of relapses have occurred when a person was angry at someone else.

7. *Lack of sleep.* Tired and irritable people lose control and relapse.

8. *Loneliness.* Strong recovery must involve remaining connected to people socially and emotionally. Make plans to prevent extended periods of loneliness.

9. *Self-pity.* In aftercare and recovery groups, people have to be reminded not to indulge in pity parties. Feeling sorry for themselves often leads to thinking they deserve a drink or drugs. The opposite of self-pity is gratitude. Grateful people do not return to alcohol or drugs.

10. *Overconfidence.* People relapse because they think they are exceptions to the rules. They believe they don't need to go to meetings or hear lectures. They also think they can be around other people who drink or do drugs. Some adults even tend bar while others drink. These are acts of overconfidence, and they always spell trouble.

These threats can be countered. But people in recovery are often blind to their reality, so they need to be confronted by a concerned person. Your child may not want to listen to your suggestions, however, just because you're the parent. Thus, it is important that early in the recovery process your child find a sponsor—another recovering person who can hold him or her accountable for attending meetings, completing assignments, and staying clean. A sponsor must not be afraid to confront your child with the reality of the situation. He or she must know the threats to recovery and discuss them with your child. The sponsor understands the cravings and struggles and is there for your child to call, day or night, when facing the temptation to relapse. He or she also provides a model of successful recovery. Finding a sponsor is encouraged in most 12-step recovery programs.

Relapse is not just one incidence of out-of-control behavior. It is not just the return to drugs and alcohol. It is a shift in attitude and actions that starts a predictable, downhill progression. That progression can be interrupted and recovery salvaged before it is too late. But to notice and intervene, you must be actively involved in your child's recovery. Attend meetings, read recovery materials, and find a support group for yourself. Being active requires sacrifice, but that sacrifice is minimal compared to the pain of watching kids bounce in and out of treatment centers. Your child needs you in the recovery process. Your love and assistance are the most powerful protection against relapse.

If relapse does occur, it is not the end of the world or the end of recovery. If handled well, it can be the beginning of long-term sobriety. Often kids need to press the limits to determine the line between the freedom to act and the need to preserve sobriety. Discovering the limitations may be all it takes to turn them toward a process of total recovery. Remember, many people who have a heart attack have relapses. All sorts of problems subject the person to relapse. Don't lose hope or give up. Instead, forgive and move quickly to return adolescents to the recovery process. Your child needs you more than ever.

Tough Love—The Key to Recovery

Jerry ended treatment for drug addiction at age 16. The day he left the treatment center to go back into the big bad world, he relapsed. On his seventeenth birthday he entered a stricter program. He didn't last two weeks before he was back out, partying as if he had never been to treatment.

Jerry's parents hurt deeply. They wanted to protect him from more harm, but they also knew true love must be tough. So they stuck to his recovery plan, which said, "If Jerry goes back into a substance-abuse lifestyle, we (his parents) will not welcome him back into our home unless he will reenter a treatment facility."

After six tries in and out of treatment, he crawled back to his parents and said, "This time it will work." Today Jerry is a certified drug- and alcohol-treatment-center counselor, making a difference in the lives of other recovering addicts. His parents' choice to administer a tough kind of love and stick to the recovery plan saved him.

Chapter 14

Preventing Drug and Alcohol Abuse: Parents Set the Tone

If I had it to do over, I would have looked for help earlier. We would have put together a plan to possibly prevent the heartaches we've experienced from Lauren's drug addiction. We just kept wishing it away, and it kept getting worse.

—Lauren's mom

When I was Taylor's age, I never heard of kids ditching school to take drugs and drink. Maybe I was naive, but I don't think it happened as often. Chemical abuse scares me to death because I have no idea what to do.

—Taylor's father

If I had the knowledge and skills to talk with my children, I think I could help them. Frankly, I don't know how to approach them.

—Mother of three

Janet's problems with drugs and alcohol took us completely by surprise. We assumed her church youth group and school would teach her everything she needed to know to stay away from substance abuse. She was the "perfect child"—active in church, a good student, and so compliant when it came to obeying us.

—Janet's mom

Parenting can feel overwhelming at times! You sometimes think the battle is too difficult, the victories too few. You start to think you can't do anything to help your children make good decisions. *Heredity or fate,* you tell yourself, *has already determined the outcome of my kids' futures.* You have tried most of the methods you've found in magazines and books, and those techniques sounded great, but they didn't work for your children.

Take heart; don't give up. You can help your children achieve a bright future full of choices. By your actions, you can help them avoid a multitude of problems, including alcoholism and drug addiction. No plan is foolproof. But we believe that the information and ideas presented in this book can provide your kids with the greatest opportunity to grow up clean. As parents, we can't prevent problems in 100 percent of the cases, but we *can* radically decrease the likelihood of drug use by our children. As you implement this plan, we believe you will see hoped-for changes in your children that will enable them to avoid the destructive behaviors you have prayed they will resist.

You Set the Pace

As we've said before, your example is the most important tool for preventing your children from using drugs and alcohol. Studies show that many factors influence teens' drug-use decisions, but that parental attitudes and actions influence them most. So ask yourself the following questions:

- Is your medicine cabinet full of mood-altering chemicals?
- Do you medicate yourself with prescription drugs or alcohol anytime you feel distress or pain?
- Do you routinely need an after-work drink or an after-dinner smoke?
- Do you hang on to prescription drugs just in case, rather than throw them out when the problem subsides?
- Do you laugh at drunken behavior on television or in movies?

- Do you wear, or allow to be worn, T-shirts or caps that have drug-related images or alcohol advertisements?
- Does the music in the house glamorize or trivialize drug or alcohol use?
- Do you lack respect for the law and refuse to observe driving regulations?

If you find yourself answering yes to most of these questions, you need to make some changes for you to be the most effective prevention tool possible.

The key to being an effective prevention tool is being a "parent in process." This means you don't claim to have all the answers. It means you are willing to admit to your children when you have made mistakes. By word and deed, you convey the idea that in your family everyone is growing, making mistakes, confessing those errors, learning from the experience, and receiving encouragement to try again.

Living Authentically in Our Children's Presence

It's no secret that kids "learn what they live," so never underestimate the power of authentically living the truth in front of your children.

For example, one of the most effective ways to teach your children effective communication skills is to model them with your spouse. Be quick to listen, slow to speak, and even slower to anger. Make it a priority to really listen to your spouse. Be sure your kids "catch you in the act" of modeling this kind of behavior as often as possible.

Now, imagine that the standard in your home is that whenever one of you needs to work late, the other receives notification as soon as the situation arises. A phone call, voice mail, text message, email, or Instant Message is acceptable—it just has to take place. Well, suppose one evening, the work has really piled up for you and you're going to need to stay late at work...only you forgot to call your spouse to let him or her know of the change in your schedule. When you arrive home, it's obvious that your spouse is not pleased—and rightfully so because you blew it big time. Of course you're going to ask your spouse for forgiveness—hopefully sooner than later. But think of the impact your apology will have if you ask for forgiveness *in front of your kids!* By acting this way in front of them, you give them the gift of knowing starting over is allowed and encouraged.

When Emotions Are Stronger Than Their Judgment

Often children make irrational decisions based on impulse. This is typical of a first drink. Under pressure, they succumb. If they have been raised in an atmosphere of rigidity, they may feel trapped in the behavior—although they want to stop—because children who never see their parents admit mistakes tend to feel they can't turn back from bad decisions. Fear of punishment if the wrong is confessed will also motivate kids to justify the action rather than admit to it, be free from the guilt, and move on. So show your children how to make good decisions. And when you make poor ones, be willing to admit them, learn from them, and go forward.

This is an area I (Jim) am working on with my family. Cathy says I sometimes come across as having a "holier than thou" attitude, especially around the kids. So lately, when it is bedtime and we pray with the girls, I have been discussing some of my struggles. I am amazed how our prayer time has changed as a result. When I am vulnerable, they are vulnerable. When I am closed, they are closed. Now instead of praying only for Aunt Karen's hemorrhoids and all the missionaries in the universe, we also pray for sincere personal needs. I have found that our prayer time has also become a miniature family support group meeting.

The Danger of Boredom

You will also be a more effective prevention tool if you are an active participant in life. Boredom is a big factor in the decision to use drugs. If parents' lives are boring, children are apt to lead boring lives as well. Kids need to see that life is full of fun things to do. Resist the urge to come home from work and slowly turn into a couch potato. Instead, show your children how to have fun. Hobbies, music, church involvement, art, sports, and exercise are all ways for parents to model alternatives to drug abuse. Take the initiative to stay active with your kids.

The Power of Being There

As we mentioned earlier, children regard their parents' very presence in a room with them as a significant sign of caring. Your children need large doses of your time, interaction, playing, questioning, studying, praying, and just being you. Whether your children let you know or not, they crave your affection, love your attention, and seek your guidance. Even in the most rebellious times, your children are begging for you to reach them. Listen to them and empathize with their problems. Offer solutions when asked for and when possible—and be a part of these solutions. Be sure they know you will always make time for them.

A teenage girl who used to babysit for us told me (Jim), "My dad seldom spends any time just with me. But when he does, he always takes me to do 'grown-up' things. Sometimes I wish we could just go to a park. He thinks it has to be an extravaganza. I'd rather have more alone times together than the twice-a-year big events. Sometimes I still want to just crawl up on his lap and have him hold me like he used to do."

God's Standards Bring Liberty

Unfortunately, the secularization of values has left today's kids without standards, but God's standards are still best. Too many young people picture God as the great killjoy in the sky instead of their strongest ally who loves them unconditionally and whose deepest desire is for their best.

Some may call us naive or simplistic, but in our experience, people who pursue a personal relationship with Jesus Christ have a better chance of staying clear of drugs and alcohol than those who don't. It is true, as the statistics quoted earlier show, that little difference exists between churched kids and unchurched kids when it comes to drug and alcohol use. Other significant studies seem to indicate, however, that those who are not merely members but who *practice their faith* in tangible ways have less difficulty resisting drugs and alcohol.[1]

The same studies reveal that kids whose parents—especially dads—have a visible, active spiritual life are less prone to drug and alcohol abuse. Strong personal faith on the part of parents and kids is a great "prevention tool."

"Breaking a Rule" or "Missing the Mark"?

In the New Testament, the word for "sin," translated literally from the original Greek, does not mean "to break a rule." Sin means "to miss the mark." Sin occurs when a person does not measure up to his or her full potential. Isn't that the biggest danger for most of our kids who drink and use drugs? The chemicals cause the kids to miss the mark, destroying their ability to achieve their goals. People are afraid to moralize the drug problem in our society, but that is exactly what is needed. The moral person is moving toward a higher mark. But most people don't know what the mark is for their lives, much less that they have missed it.

Drug-Proofing with God's Help

One reason many kids decide not to use drugs or alcohol is that they believe it would dishonor God. You won't find that information in most books on drug and alcohol prevention, but when abstinent kids were asked why they chose to stay clean, that's what they said. Others said they believed their bodies were the temples of God and that to use chemicals would be dishonoring to Him. Clearly, children's belief in God and the value they place on Him are determinants in their decisions about drug and alcohol usage.

That God is left out of much prevention material is ironic

because mention of Him saturates the literature on treatment. The first three steps in a 12-step program have addicted persons admit they cannot handle the problem alone, acknowledge God can handle it, and allow God to take control of their lives. We don't know of one treatment program in the country that doesn't use these principles. Doesn't it make sense that if God is integral in recovering from addiction, He should also be integral in preventing addiction problems?

Unconditional Love

Drug-proof kids are kids who are loved. They know that whether they have been good or bad, destructive or constructive, they are loved unconditionally. Their parents don't always feel thrilled to be their parents. Many times we have become discouraged or irritated, and at times we have seriously considered trading our kids in for other models. But that does not alter our love for them, a fact we try to emphasize often in both word and action.

Conditional love comes with strings attached. It implies that if you act a certain way or do certain things, love will be given. Children often have a sense that if they mess up too badly, the love will go away. When children feel the uncertainty of conditional love, they are challenged to see how bad they can be and still receive love. This is a way of determining their basic worth. Rather than being motivated to greatness so as not to lose their parents' love, they are motivated toward delinquency, including alcohol and drugs. While bordering on the edge of rejection by parents, they seek acceptance in other places, often with peer groups.

You cannot win with children if they are not guaranteed your love. Drugs and alcohol produce an instant gratification that some children in a love vacuum come to crave. Fill your kids' needs for love and acceptance with great floods of unconditional love.

Behavior and Discipline

Children's behavior should be channeled from an early age.

Unconditional love does not imply a lack of discipline—in fact, it's just the opposite. Love means disciplining kids for their own good even when it is painful or inconvenient for the parent. This is because children left to their own whims can be counted on to make poor decisions. But through discipline and encouragement, they learn the boundaries of responsible behavior and the consequences of irresponsible conduct. They discover the value of delayed gratification rather than demand instant pleasure. As they are led into responsible decisions, they learn to ensure that the long-term results of their choices are not destructive and to consider more than just the initial effects of a decision. And that helps them say no to drugs and alcohol too.

Practically, this means irresponsible behavior must bring undesirable consequences, such as increased restrictions. This teaches the principle of cause and effect. If children's performances in school deteriorate, time spent on the telephone could be cut down or eliminated. A driver's license might be taken away. Curfew might be shortened, and time spent with a friend could be cut down.

Parents and their children should establish the rules of the house together. Discipline is most effective if children know the consequences of irresponsible behavior before they act. It is better yet if they themselves suggest the consequences. But you, as the parent, must follow through and apply the consequences.

A Case Study Involving Consequences

A while ago, I (Jim) had a mother and son come into my office. They had many problems, but one was that the son kept staying out past his curfew. His mother had threatened and screamed, but nothing had changed. I asked the 16-year-old boy, "Do you think your curfew is unfair?"

"Not really, except on special occasions when I want to stay out an hour longer," he replied.

"How about if your mom compromises and gives you 15 more minutes on certain weeknights and half an hour more on weekends?"

I asked. "She must always know where you are, and if you call, she'll give you a 10-minute grace period."

He smiled and said, "Sounds great to me."

I then asked, "What should the consequences be if you're late for curfew or don't let your mom know where you are?"

He looked at his mom and answered, "That's her department."

"Not necessarily," I said. "You seem like an intelligent person with a desire to please your mom. What would you suggest as a consequence if we can get your mom to agree to the new terms?"

His suggested consequences were stricter than his mother or I would have proposed, so I helped them modify the restrictions. But we had successfully involved him in establishing the restrictions. He knew the consequences; after all, they were his idea. I suggested that if, after six months, he proved he could be trusted, they renegotiate the "contract" and give him more freedom. If he continued in his irresponsible behavior, less freedom would be the result.

The tendency for many parents is to protect their kids from the consequences of behavior. Seeking love and acceptance themselves, or out of some other unresolved need, parents often rescue children when the best course would be to let them feel the pain that grows out of an irresponsible decision. Without discipline, children remain immature and problems flourish. A tough kind of love is hard to administer, but it is greatly needed if children are to be taught responsibility.

Consistency Is Key

Too often parents are inconsistent in handling irresponsible behavior. One time they are extremely strict, but on the next offense they take a more liberal approach. Sometimes one parent sabotages the discipline of the other. The first parent properly restricts behavior after an irresponsible act, while the second parent goes behind the other's back and allows the child some privileges. This inconsistency encourages irresponsibility and arrests development. Parents must be as unified as possible in their approach to discipline.

I (Steve) worked with a boy whose stepfather continually sabotaged the mother's discipline. The stepfather wanted to win the boy's approval, but the boy didn't like the man any better in spite of his leniency. Instead, the son manipulated the man to get what he wanted. The inconsistency not only produced an irresponsible child, but it also kept him from getting needed treatment for a terrible addiction.

Let Your Kids Blame You

When parents inform children that any use of alcohol or drugs will produce an immediate restriction, they give their kids a great tool for countering peer pressure. When approached with the opportunity to do drugs, a child can respond, "If my dad finds out I've smoked a joint, he'll take away my driver's license for six months. I just can't risk it for one high." Lines similar to these have been employed many times to withstand the pressure to use drugs or alcohol.

Just as irresponsible behavior should bring greater restrictions, so responsible behavior should bring greater rewards. Help children see the long-term benefits of responsible decisions by providing some short-term evidence. It is hard for kids to understand (or care) that practicing responsible decision-making while they are young leads to responsible, rewarding decisions when they are older. Provide them with motivation through a consistent plan of rewards and trust.

The Right Kind of Motivation

Once when my daughter Christy was in elementary school, my wife was showing me (Jim) Christy's most recent report card. It was outstanding—definitely better than any I ever brought home. Yet my first reaction was to look at the B+ grade and say, "I wonder why she didn't get an A?" After Cathy and I talked about it we decided to take Christy out for an ice cream sundae and celebrate her wonderful report card. I had to resist my urge to pass over all the outstanding grades and concentrate on the few that, while still excellent, were not perfect.

This system of rewards and restrictions prepares children for the real world. When a person takes a job, a predetermined salary has been set, and expectations of performance are communicated. But if the person is responsible and does outstanding work, he or she has the opportunity for promotion and a raise or bonus. Starting early to help your children understand this system prepares them for later life. But the most important thing it does is provide motivation to achieve beyond the level of mediocrity. It is another reason to make good choices.

Control

One of the hot buttons of adolescence is control. Who is going to be in charge: Will it be the parents or the child? The answer develops from an ongoing negotiation between parents and kids. In the healthiest of families, this tension is a difficult part of adjusting to the growth of the children. Kids always want more control, and most parents want to retain it themselves.

In unhealthy families, parents go to extremes. They try to be either overly controlling or too permissive. Overly controlling parents are afraid to let go of the children, which sets up the children for rebellion. And one way the rebellion is manifested is to use forbidden substances. Permissive parents tend to have low self-esteem and need their children as friends for support. They set up a peer relationship rather than a parent–child relationship. This lends itself to drug abuse because they have established no boundaries. It also produces insecure children because they have to set their own limits and usually are not mature enough to do so.

In a healthy situation where drug prevention is a priority, control should be handed over to children when they prove to be responsible. The underlying principle is that when children learn to protect themselves, parents have less need to protect. Young children need protection because they are easily victimized. But as kids grow older, they should learn how to prevent being victimized by exercising self-control.

Control is a prevention issue because alcohol and other drugs place children in danger of losing control. Children under the influence of drugs are in grave peril. They must be taught the following dangers of losing control:

- Death due to driving while intoxicated or under the influence of drugs
- Overdose (it is always a gamble as to whether street drugs are in reality what the seller said they were)
- Getting pregnant or making someone pregnant while drunk or high
- Diseases such as herpes and AIDS that are either terminal or destroy a normal sex life forever.

The Importance of Learning Self-Control

In Titus 2:2, God commands us to teach older men to be self-controlled. If the older men demonstrate this trait to their sons and daughters, the younger generation too will learn the value of being in control. One of my (Steve's) friends gave up drinking years ago because of this scriptural principle. He believed that to honor God, a person must be under the Spirit's control, not under the influence of a chemical.

Any child who comes home drunk or stoned is obviously not in control. When the situation occurs, the parents must step in and resume the protective control the child is not able to maintain. Because the child will resist giving up independence, he or she will try to manipulate the parents into weakening their position. But it is crucial that consistency and tough love prevail.

Contracts

Contracts governing children's behavior can be controversial. We don't advise them for every situation. When it comes to drugs, however, they work well. Contracting for appropriate behavior can also be good preparation for the adult world, where people frequently contract for jobs to be done and behavior levels to be met. When kids are 12 or 13 years old, you can begin using a form similar to the one below:

Family Contract

In an effort to work well as a family and offer ourselves as an example for other families, I agree to the following:

1. I will not use or experiment with drugs.
2. I will not drink or make a decision about drinking until I am of legal age.
3. I will attend school unless I am sick or with the family.

If the contract is broken:

- First time results in weekend restriction.
- Second time results in I must stay away from participating friends for two weeks.
- Third time results in attending family counseling.

_____

Son or Daughter

_____

Father

_____

Mother

_____

Date

This contract is a basic example. You will want to write your own that relates to your specific needs. The contract can be reviewed and altered at regular intervals. It provides a point of discussion and objective measure of behavior. Children must look their parents in the eyes and say, "I have upheld my end of the contract." As children grow older, the contract should include the following: never ride with someone who is intoxicated or using drugs; never date someone who uses alcohol or drugs; call to be picked up rather than ride with someone under the influence.

Besides ensuring that children know their parents' expectations, contracts can help motivate kids to say no to negative pressure.

Know Your Kids, Know Their Friends

Several years ago the CBS program *48 Hours* showed two days in the lives of teenagers attending and some not attending school. These were contrasting portraits of kids who did well in school and those who were skipping school to hang out at a local pizza place. The principal of the inner-city school obviously loved the kids and was involved in their lives. Rather than sitting behind a desk, he roamed the halls. He went out on the streets to encourage the truants to return. During the show he said he had only one piece of advice for parents: "Know who your child's friends are."

As mentioned earlier, studies reveal that one of the highest determinants for drug use is whether children have friends who use drugs. If your kids hang out with friends who are using marijuana, your children probably use marijuana. Scripture tells us, "Do not be misled: 'Bad company corrupts good character'" (1 Corinthians 15:33). It happens every time.

Open Your Home

Know your children's friends. Don't let your kids spend time with someone you don't know. A minimum requirement should be that your children's friends must come to your house before your children are allowed to go out with them. Let your kids know their friends are always welcome for dinner. Encourage your children to bring friends home; let your house be one of those places where kids like to come. Don't be so restrictive or intolerant that your children's friends feel uncomfortable in your home.

One parent had a big hole at the bottom of his bedroom door. He was proud of that hole because some neighborhood kid kicked it in while playing football in the hall. "You shouldn't let kids trash your house," he said, "but that hole is there because my house was a place where kids loved to come. I know I wasn't perfect as a father, but so far my 18-year-old son has chosen not to drink or take drugs. I knew who his friends were, and they knew me."

What If You Don't Like Their Friends?

If your children have less-than-desirable friends, refusing access to them will produce anger and bitterness. But you have a responsibility to restrict access to their negative-influence friends. Deciding when and where your child spends time with those friends is your prerogative as the parent, especially if you have conclusive evidence the friends are drug users or drinkers. But more important than restricting access to such friends is communicating your concerns to your children. Tell them why you are troubled by the decision to have these particular people as friends. A poor choice of friends should provide a teachable moment.

When Your Neighborhood Is Unhealthy

It is common to hear adults in Alcoholics Anonymous say they tried to solve their problems by moving to a new community, and it didn't work. It might, however, be a more effective solution for kids. Sometimes a child becomes deeply involved in an unhealthy subculture at a particular school. All the child's friends may be drug users. The child is caught using drugs or alcohol, and the parents have to decide what to do to save the child. The best choice in such a case may be to remove the child from that particular subculture by moving the family. We know of a father who took his sons from Dallas, Texas, to Nashville, Tennessee, for this reason, and it truly helped.

Moving is not a cure-all or a quick-fix solution, but it can be a vital part of a plan to save a child. Nothing is more important in drug prevention than helping kids choose their friends. Channel children toward healthy peer relationships, and you will be taking a giant step toward prevention of drug and alcohol usage.

Using Drugs to Cope with Pain

Alcohol and drugs are used to cope with pain. Escape into a bottle is a common American custom. "I need a drink" is a common phrase in movies. It's no wonder our kids turn to chemicals to cope with pressure, loneliness, and insecurity. They are simply playing follow the leader. Adults have made escape acceptable in kids' eyes. Broken marriages and out-of-control spending are examples of people using escape as a way to cope. Television role models escape behavior as well. And if parents can't cope, children won't be able to either.

The subtle message from all these escapist practices is that the goal in life is to get by, to avoid negatives. We need to help our kids see that struggling to hang in there is successful living. We must help our kids find positive methods of coping, but we must also recognize that life's beauty is found beyond the coping mechanisms. A coping mechanism should produce a better life when the coping is done. Drinking makes you depressed, and the next day you will drink again. Running, on the other hand, relaxes you and makes you lose some fat. Drugs medicate your loneliness today and leave you addicted tomorrow. But reading relaxes your mind today and makes you smarter tomorrow. These positive alternatives move children beyond coping and into a better life.

Healthy Outlets for Emotional Overload

Kids who don't use alcohol or other drugs have found creative and productive alternatives. Their parents created an environment that fostered competency and growth in a variety of areas. The following are some of the areas into which kids can channel their energies.

Groups. Rather than being expected to form couples, kids should be encouraged to have fun and to mature in group settings. This is why a great church youth ministry is important. If the youth ministry has a strong program, it will have plenty of group activities. Camps, retreats, social gatherings, and Bible studies are strong drug-prevention tools.

Sports. Active participation in sports has many benefits. Children can obtain positive recognition, develop discipline, and accomplish things on their own. The group becomes the team and creates its own pressure to work and win. Sports also help a child stay fit, which in turn helps maintain strong self-esteem. Athletic competencies stay with a child for a lifetime. Parents need to be willing to sacrifice by making extra automobile trips—including some carpool nightmares—so their children are encouraged to compete. I (Jim) am convinced one of the major reasons I did not abuse drugs was my involvement in athletics.

Arts. Early signs of talent should be encouraged in your children. Buy a secondhand piano. Purchase a set of oil or acrylic paints. Sing as a family. Offer lessons. We encourage taking a class together whenever possible. This will help build a powerful bond between you and your kids.

Hobbies. Collecting is fun for many people. Don't wait for your children to discover stamp or coin collecting. Get them started, and see if the hobby catches on. Spare time is best spent with some productive activity kids can be proud of and call their own. Encourage any areas of interest your children show.

Community involvement. Today's children are self-absorbed. They see things only in terms of what they can do for themselves or how they can make themselves feel. As an antidote, involve your children with projects that assist others. Encourage them to help fellow students with their studies. Take them to nursing homes, hospitals, and homeless shelters to visit and help out. Get them out of themselves and into the lives of others.

Negative Peer Pressure

Oftentimes kids will become involved with alcohol and other drugs because they're not equipped to deal with the peer pressure to try them. The word "no" is a powerful device for resisting pressure and avoiding a lifetime of misery. Teach your children to say no. Show them how to display strength in the face of pressure. Encourage them to flee the temptations of youth. Use some creative examples of ways to say no. For example, when asked if they want a drink, kids can reply:

- "I'd have a drink, but I get sick, and I wouldn't want to throw up in your car."
- "That's not my brand."
- "That's not my year."
- "In my family, we just don't drink. It's a tradition."
- "I think I'm allergic to it."
- "My parents will take away my license."

The ability to say no is the ultimate weapon against peer pressure. (See the "Just Say No" game at the end of this book for ways to help your kids turn down drugs.) Teaching kids to say no is helpful, but showing how through example is the best way for them to learn to use no effectively. Children need to see their parents—you—say no to:

- Food while on a diet
- A drink when everyone else is drinking
- A car that is too expensive
- Clothes that would throw off the budget
- A movie below the standards of acceptability
- An activity that interferes with a previous commitment

You won't be able to help your children offer resistance under pressure until you can withstand pressure yourself. You won't teach them to say no until you can say it yourself.

You have the opportunity and responsibility to shape your children's choices and behaviors. Your commitment to them is your most valuable prevention tool against alcohol and other drugs. It teaches your kids to live up to that commitment through the tough times. Modeling behavior that goes beyond mediocrity is not easy. You have to look inward to find the areas that need improvement and the will to improve those areas. In the midst of trying new techniques for prevention, never forget that *you* are your most effective prevention tool.

Chapter 15

Motivating Others to Drug-Proof Their Kids

In Albuquerque, New Mexico, a group of parents have banded together to curb drug abuse and provide treatment for kids who need help. Their organization is called "Parents Against Drugs," and they have approached the city with an innovative idea. When a child is caught possessing drugs or alcohol at school, he or she would be transferred to another school where everyone enrolled is dealing with the same struggle. The students would provide tremendous support for each other to stay drug free. Abstinence would be a constant school goal. This would give access to a "treatment program" to many kids who normally would not be able to receive quality help. It would also be much less expensive than most official treatment facilities.

These parents may not succeed in getting the school established, but they have gained the ear of the community and its officials.

In Fort Worth, Texas, various sectors of the community are pulling together to do something about drunk driving. Businesses, parents, PTAs, and anonymous groups have joined in a cooperative effort to reduce drunk driving deaths on New Year's Eve. Free rides home are provided to those who get drunk.

In Philadelphia, parents became angry watching the crack dealers move into the heart of their neighborhoods. They refused to sit back and be invaded by drug pushers. As a result, their group is one of the best informed in the country about drugs. Law enforcement agencies trained the parents how to observe behavior the way police do, identifying actions consistent with drug pushing and dealing. Now, as trained observers, they have credibility when they call the police with a complaint about a drug dealer on the street.

Because these parents learned how to spot the problem and took action when they did, they have totally cleaned up some neighborhoods that were infested with crack and its dealers. When parents decide to do something about a problem, they can have a tremendous influence in a community.

If you have been frustrated with the lack of progress in your community about drug and alcohol abuse, you are not alone. Thousands of parents across the country have become disgusted as they have watched their communities deteriorate and their children be destroyed. Many of these parents have banded together to form groups such as those mentioned. They stopped expecting someone else to solve the problem and decided to do something themselves. We believe it is time parents stop pointing fingers and start looking for ways everyone in a community can help to stop chemical abuse.

Parent Power

When parents pull together to save their kids and protect their community, they often succeed, as illustrated by the preceding examples. But such efforts must start with someone. One concerned parent has to be willing to take the initiative for drug-free kids. In every case where a community has turned around its drug problem, the process began with one person who decided to rally the other parents. You can be that person. You can be responsible for changing the lives of thousands of young people and saving a community.

Form a Community Advisory Board

One of the best ways to motivate others is to form a community advisory board. The purpose of such a board is to inform and educate people of the hazards of drug and alcohol abuse and to act on the information. One board in New Jersey put together flyers that give parents discussion-starter questions to use in talking with their children. They organized a telephone hot line and parent seminars, and they chaperoned school dances.

You can start an advisory board just by asking people to serve or you can join an existing organization. We suggest you call a newspaper reporter and ask for a story to be written that announces the first board meeting. An advisory board should include prominent members of the community—physicians, nurses, and others from the medical community; educators and leaders in parent–teacher groups; pastors and church youth workers; professionals from the treatment field who understand addiction; and leaders from civic groups such as Rotary and Kiwanis. Perhaps the most important contributors are the parents in the community, who should be invited to come and express their concerns to the group.

Lobby at the City Council

Many communities have an active city council that is willing to listen to people. In such cases, rather than forming an advisory board, you might choose to organize parents to lobby the city council, asking it to pass helpful laws or fund treatment programs. This approach might require going door-to-door to ask parents to come to a meeting, but if they will come in large enough numbers, most city officials will be accommodating. Forming an advisory board or organizing parents to approach the city council can be the first important step in a grassroots effort to change the direction of the drug problem.

Ensure Existing Laws Are Strictly Enforced

Parents can take many other steps. One of the most effective is to ensure that existing laws are strictly enforced in the community. Police frequently complain that it does no good to arrest people if the judge is going to put them back on the street. Mothers Against Drunk Driving (MADD) did a wonderful thing when they began to monitor judges who sentenced people convicted of driving under the influence of alcohol. Lenient judges, under pressure and exposure, started to take DUIs more seriously. Because of MADD's efforts, progress is being made against drunk driving for the first time in our nation's history.

Your group may likewise want to approach a judge or two about their leniency and how that affects your children. Encourage strict enforcement of the laws forbidding drug dealing, drug using, and drinking by minors.

Form Intervention Groups on School Campuses

School systems are ripe for innovative programs. Every time a school system organizes to attack the problem, many lives are diverted from the path of addiction. Parents can volunteer to form intervention groups in the schools. If children are caught possessing alcohol or drugs, they can be referred to a committee that assesses the problem and recommends or demands action. The committee can send kids to counseling or treatment centers, require them to attend special courses on alcohol and drugs, or insist that kids be separated from other kids who use chemicals. Many schools have set up such committees that consist of parents, teachers, and school administrators.

Several years go I (Jim) was asked to speak at a public high school assembly in Whittier, California, on the subject of "Making Decisions About Drugs and Alcohol." The assembly was sponsored by the school's PTA, and the program was well received. The leader of the PTA told me ahead of time that I was free to mention my belief that people can have a personal relationship with Jesus Christ and that He cares about the chemically addicted.

After the assembly I asked this wonderful woman how she got involved in presenting these programs. She told me she had attended her first PTA meeting the previous year. The group had been apathetic. They budgeted $8,000 for "prevention" assemblies, but no one wanted to invest the time needed to organize them, so no assemblies had been planned.

The night after that PTA meeting, she couldn't sleep. It bothered her that this group had the opportunity to influence kids in a positive way but didn't have the energy. The next day she volunteered to be in charge of the assemblies. In the first year, she presented programs on drugs and alcohol, setting standards, sexual abuse, peer pressure, and pregnancy crises. The students loved the new approach, and after each assembly the speaker would invite interested kids to another room to talk. I met with more than 50 students who wanted to talk about their drug and alcohol problems the day I spoke. This one woman's decision to invest her time in the PTA was richly rewarded.

An Investment of Your Time

It's amazing how much we, as concerned parents and youth leaders, can do to help steer our kids and their friends from drug and alcohol addiction simply by showing up and getting involved. Doug Fields and Jim Hancock are two church youth workers who volunteer to sit on drug-abuse committees. They've had many opportunities to make presentations to junior high and high school students simply because they volunteered. You can do the same!

When money is available, parents can motivate their cities to do some creative and helpful things. New treatment centers can be built. When treatment beds are available, the courts can use alternative sentencing programs. Rather than sending kids to jail on a first offense, judges can mandate them into treatment programs. Also, innovative prevention programs can be set up in schools, along with procedures for intervention at the first sign of an abuse problem.

Just as parental prevention revolves around increasing rewards or restrictions based on children's conduct, so can school-based prevention programs. One reward is scholarship money. A fund could be established for those children who finish school and have no record of a drug or alcohol violation and who affirm, having obtained five supporting statements from others, that they have not used drugs or alcohol. This is expensive and extreme, but it could motivate some kids not to use drugs or alcohol.

Develop Tough Laws

The restriction side of the prevention program must have some severe penalties. Judges must be willing to restrict freedom and privileges. If judges are strict, many kids will be deterred from becoming involved in drugs or alcohol. Parents should also work to get state laws changed so that any minor caught driving while intoxicated or on drugs or selling drugs from a car would automatically have his or her driver's license suspended for one year. This is an effective restriction to use with adolescents. Adolescents may not sense the reality of prison, but they can feel the effect of going a year without driving.

Parents can also band together to hold each other accountable to uphold the laws. First they must agree that alcohol and drugs are unacceptable at all school functions and community parties for teenagers. Any function that includes drinking and drugging should be shut down, and those responsible should be arrested. Parents also need to agree to let the offenders stay in jail and not bail them out instantly.

But more important, parents need to agree that any parent supplying or allowing kids access to alcohol will be turned in and prosecuted for contributing to the delinquency of minors. Too many efforts of concerned parents are sabotaged by other parents who don't understand the dangers of alcohol and drugs. Don't let such a parent get away with harming your children. We have seen too many lives ruined because someone did not want to offend another adult.

Begin a Support Group for Parents

Parents who have the potential to harm your kids can be helped in support groups. Such a group will provide guidance to those who struggle with kids using drugs. It offers a place where they can ask questions of other parents about drug prevention or some problem that has surfaced in their families.

The support group can also encourage people who don't have

children with a drug problem but just need a place to express their discouragement in the fight against chemical abuse.

You don't have to be a counselor or psychologist to run a support group. Just post notices in appropriate places, informing people about the purpose of the group. When the first person comes, you have begun a support group that could be the nucleus for the drug-proof movement in your community and a major source of parent power.

Drug-Free Zones, Neighborhood Watch, Curfew

Many communities now have Drug-Free Zones around schools where vendors cannot sell alcohol, tobacco, or other drugs within a certain mile radius of a school campus. Some communities participate in an active Neighborhood Watch Program. Almost any police agency in the United States and Canada will help you put together a Neighborhood Watch Program in your community. Neighborhood Watch, whether it be a community-based program or your own prevention, helps you look out for other families and friends. Recently in our neighborhood, a car with two suspicious-looking strangers inside kept driving around the block very slowly. Our neighbors called us and asked if we recognized them. We didn't, so our neighbors called the police. The officers stopped the two men and found out that it was an innocent driving lesson, but the officer thanked us for our concern and told us we did the right thing. Didn't someone once say, "Better safe than sorry"?

As several communities in America institute curfew laws for young people, no one is touting the curfew crackdown as a panacea for drug abuse, crime, and violence. Many problems occur, however, when kids are in the wrong place at the wrong time. Inglewood, California, is a rather rough community just outside downtown Los Angeles. The chief of Inglewood's police department once said, "I want young people off the streets. If I have them off the streets, they will not likely be the victims of crime or perpetrators of crime."

If your community does not have a curfew for teenagers, perhaps it's time to help it get started. One major city adopted a pilot program that served as a model for other cities to follow. Curfew is at 10:00 at night, seven nights a week, for youths ages 15 and under, and midnight for 16- and 17-year-olds. Violators are cited and taken to centers staffed by police and recreation workers until the parents arrive and pick them up. In the first two years of this program, violent crimes and drug abuse involving older teenagers were down significantly.

Know where your kids are at all times. As a parent, you aren't always running a popularity contest. If you don't know where your teenagers are, they could be an easier target of violence and drug abuse. Create family policies as early in the teen years as possible that require your children to call you whenever they are moving from one place to another. You have better judgment than a 16-year-old.

Positive Peer Influence

Before you motivate the parents to band together, you may want to get the kids together. When children become involved in positive, peer-influence groups, it is usually easy to motivate their parents to help the community fight drugs and alcohol. When peer groups of this nature form, they are based on a pledge by all the members to each other and to their parents to remain drug free.

This might sound naive for many who live in the inner city. It's not. Many kids want to belong to something worthwhile and meaningful. They join a gang or a drug-using group of friends because of a lack of alternatives. A group of positive peer supporters could be the key to a drug-free life. We are encouraged by the many Students Against Drunk Driving (SADD) groups in schools across the country.

Positive Influence, Powerful Results

In one major city in the Southeast, kids have banded together under the leadership of their parents. They have formed a patrol group to go through the town and look for suspicious behavior. When they see what appears to be a drug deal, they phone the police, who respond immediately. Working with the police in this way develops respect for law enforcement and an understanding of the men and women in uniform. It gives the children a sense of importance and accomplishment. It is a "hobby" that uses time productively. For many, it is the alternative they need to stay off drugs. It also brings parents together to help the kids, and motivates parents to clean up their own lives.

Another positive peer association for kids is accomplished through drama. In one town kids volunteered to perform plays about drug and alcohol abuse. In studying and acting out the parts, they started to understand more fully the feelings and consequences surrounding drug abuse. Some of the kids were former drug users, and the plays helped them understand their own problems and maintain sobriety. The plays were performed throughout the community, and hundreds of people were motivated to get involved in some manner of drug and alcohol prevention.

Whether it be drama or other activities, bring the kids in your community together in new and exciting ways. Provide them with the alternatives they need. And ask their parents to join you in your fight.

Calling the Church to Action

The war against drugs can be won when all the community comes together to help. We have seen churches play an effective part in such efforts to fight drug abuse. This is not a task to be left to the youth workers or Sunday school teachers; it is a project for the entire church. The first step in motivating a church to respond to the war against drugs is to train the staff, elected leaders, and teachers in the areas of drug education, prevention, and treatment. When a common base of knowledge is developed, the church leadership can respond in unity to help the community.

Once the church staff has been educated about drug abuse,

courses should be offered for parents. Parents need to know the facts about drugs and prevention concepts so they can relay them to their kids and support the actions of the church. When the parents have been made knowledgeable, it is time to educate the kids. Children are not educated best by lectures. Bring in a recovering addict to tell his or her story. Show films that present the realities of drug abuse in graphic form. Have other kids who have overcome the problem talk about recovery. Educate the children of your church by giving them as much exposure to the subject as possible. Be creative in designing new ways to present the information.

Getting Informed

If you are familiar with the drug-prevention resources in your community, the job of arranging good presentations will be much easier. Checking with the local Council on Alcoholism or doing an online search for agencies in your area are good places to start looking. Work with the prevention and treatment groups on educating kids and counseling those with problems. Even if these groups aren't run by people who have strong Christian principles, they possess important information and experience. In the process of working with you, they will see the church apart from the caricatures developed by the media.

One of the most helpful things a church can do is to organize a group of parents who will provide healthy activities when adolescent temptations are at a peak. Plan pizza parties for the kids after games and dances. A game night can be fun for everyone. The times when teens are most likely to get into trouble are the times when the church's creative resources can be most beneficial. Don't be afraid to work with other churches on these projects either. Pooled resources can make it possible to provide a greater variety of positive, fun-filled alternatives. The church can set the standard of leadership for the rest of the community.

Taking the 12 Steps to Church

Some Christians are skeptical of the 12-step recovery programs because the programs are usually not affiliated with a church. We are excited, however, about the large number of churches now sponsoring Alcoholics Anonymous Programs as part of their ministries.

We believe the 12 steps are in line with what the Bible teaches. Unfortunately, throughout the years, people have largely lost the true meaning of who the "higher power" represents. Dr. Vernon J. Bittner has revised the 12 steps for Christians. His desire was to reclaim the 12 steps for the church and to be specific about the identity of the "higher power":

12 Steps for Christian Living

1. We admit our need for God's gift of salvation, confessing we are powerless over certain areas of our lives and that our lives are at times sinful and unmanageable.
2. We come to believe through the Holy Spirit that a power who came in the person of Jesus Christ and who is greater than ourselves can transform our weaknesses into strengths.
3. We make a decision to turn our wills and our lives over to the care of Jesus Christ as we understand Him, hoping to understand Him more fully.
4. We make a searching and fearless moral inventory of ourselves, both our strengths and our weaknesses.
5. We admit to Christ, to ourselves, and to another human being the exact nature of our sins.
6. We become entirely ready to have Christ heal all those defects of character that prevent us from having a more spiritual lifestyle.
7. We humbly ask Christ to transform all our shortcomings.
8. We make a list of all persons we have harmed and become willing to make amends to them all.
9. We make direct amends to such persons whenever

possible, except when to do so would injure them or others.

10. We continue to take personal inventory, and when we're wrong, we promptly admit it. When we're right, we thank God for His guidance.

11. We seek through prayer and meditation to improve our conscious contact with Jesus Christ, as we understand Him, praying for knowledge of God's will for us and the power to carry that out.

12. Having experienced a new sense of spirituality as a result of these steps, and realizing this is a gift of God's grace, we are willing to share the message of Christ's love and forgiveness with others and to practice these principles for spiritual living in all our affairs.[1]

Anyone can start a movement to fight drug and alcohol abuse. The person in your community who makes the biggest difference could be you. Your action can mobilize the forces of the press, the school system, law enforcement, and parents to defeat the drug problem in your town. The drug war cannot be won alone. It requires the help of every area of the community. But one person with compassion and commitment can motivate others to begin the fight.

One housewife has made a big difference in our community. Molly Frye is the mother of three teenagers. A few years ago she got fed up with what her kids were being taught about sex and drug abuse in the school system, and she decided to do something about it. Without a day's experience in formal youth work, Molly wrote a curriculum for both crisis pregnancy and drug and alcohol abuse. As a guest instructor, she presented her curriculum in a health class. It was so well received that last year she and a modest band of volunteers spoke to more than 16,000 students. One person can make a difference!

Chapter 16

It's Never Too Late to Begin

Robert's Story

Robert was a computer genius by the age of 13. He was introduced to computers at age 12, and within two years he was writing his own programs. At age 16, one of his games was acquired and distributed by a major software publisher. Within three years, the royalties made him wealthy.

Although he had a sky-high IQ, Robert was not smart enough to stay away from drugs. In his hours-long programming marathons, he used cocaine to fuel his creativity. When he was done, he smoked marijuana to relax and come down from his creative high. It didn't take long for both his money and his drive to disappear. At age 25, he was penniless, homeless, and living on the streets of Phoenix, Arizona.

His parents put him in drug and alcohol treatment centers, psychiatric hospitals, and even sent him on a missionary work cruise. Nothing helped. The court system jailed Robert a number of times and finally gave up on him. The judge took Robert off probation and told him and his parents he could do nothing more for him. Robert would have to change or face a long prison sentence. He returned to the streets to do odd jobs, make a few dollars, and buy marijuana. Drugs always took precedence over food.

At age 28, suffering from malnutrition and pneumonia, Robert was admitted to Phoenix General Hospital. He wanted to die, and his parents expected he would. His physicians talked to him about his lack of will to live. They did everything they could to help, but nothing seemed to work. Robert weakened steadily.

When hope was but a thread, a divine intervention took place. A newly hired nurse took care of Robert one evening. She helped him bathe and perform his bodily functions. As she helped him physically, she also ministered to him spiritually. She told her own story of addiction, despair, and recovery. She talked of a loving God who had helped her find new meaning in life. She spent hours telling Robert he was not alone, he was loved, and she cared.

Somehow her words crept into Robert's empty heart and filled him with a new desire to live. In his weakness, he turned to God for strength and guidance to begin again. The subsequent process of recovery took him into drug treatment and hundreds of Alcoholics Anonymous meetings. From the brink of death was born a new life that has helped others find new hope as well. He has taken his simple message to anyone who will listen: "It's never too late to change."

Help Yourself, Help Your Children

The time to move into action is now. Whether you have young children or you have a 50-year-old "child," it is never too late to start helping with a drug or alcohol problem. If your children have already succumbed to substance abuse, it is easy to think it is hopeless.

Out of remorse, you may spend your time dwelling on the "if onlys." You say to yourself, "If only I had protected my child from the beginning." Keeping your focus on the "if onlys" or the "what ifs" only delays needed action. Rather than thinking of where you went wrong or where you could have done better, begin where you are. For years you may have rationalized that you could do nothing. Now you know that through intervention you may be able to change the course of your child's future. It will take great courage for you to act. And because magical cures are not available, it will take perseverance to alter behavior that may have existed for years.

The alternative to acting, however, is to do nothing—a choice full of misery for yourself and those you could help. It is painful to intervene in a person's life, but the pain of intervention is much less agonizing than watching an alcohol or drug problem lead a person to death or insanity. Many parents sit back and pray that something will happen to help their children. They wait for a miraculous intervention that will stop the addiction quickly and painlessly. While they sit back, however, perhaps God is calling them to move into action. Maybe He is calling you to move into action to save your own children or the children of people in your neighborhood.

You may not have children who are into drugs. Your kids may just be starting kindergarten or the first grade. You look into a pair of sweet, innocent eyes, and you question whether you should trouble this precious person with the worries of drug and alcohol abuse. It's hard to believe your children could be approached with drugs at such a young age. But for the sake of your kids and your community, please believe us: It is never too early to talk to your kids.

Use the information you now have and discuss it with your children at age four or five. Teach them how to say no when approached with magic pills or the promise that they will feel as if they are living in a fairy tale. Show them what harmful substances look like. Warn them of the actions and motives of those who offer such substances to them.

Don't Delay Getting Help

Parents of addicted kids often don't act when they should for several reasons. Some think they can handle the problem alone. They can't. Others delay getting help because they don't want to accept the finality of a diagnosis of drug addiction or alcoholism. Anything but one of those labels for their children! So the parents rely on home remedies that always fail, or they resort to quick fixes that merely put a bandage on a severe wound. Other parents wait to get help in the hope that the child is going through a phase. But the "phase" will not go away. It is locked in by the addiction process. Until the parents act, it will not get any better.

Often parents delay action because they realize they may have to face problems of their own that they have worked hard to hide. Because of scars from the past or a marriage gone sour, they become so wrapped up in their miseries that they have little time to help a child prevent potential problems. They become so numbed by their own pain that they do nothing. The focus remains on the parents' problems. Parents must find a way to work through their own difficulties and free themselves to help their children. If they don't, the struggles and pain are passed on from generation to generation.

Like Father, Like Son

A certain man had a son who was an adolescent alcoholic and a daughter who was a cocaine addict. This father spent about a year in constant worry about their problems. At the end of the day, he would leave the stress of his work to return home, where the stress and pain were much greater. The normal glass of wine he drank with dinner became a mixed drink before dinner, many glasses of wine during dinner, and drinks afterward. His tolerance was as large as his son's. Not until he took his son to an Alcoholics Anonymous meeting did he discover that what was in his son was also in himself. He started recovery alongside his son. The whole family joined in recovery because the father faced his own problem.

This example, unfortunately, is the exception. Most parents refuse to face their problems and addictions. They fail themselves and their children. It takes courage to be the exception rather than the rule.

Become a Positive Example for Your Children

You may have turned to alcohol or drugs because of the pain in your own life. Or like many others, you may have been developing an addiction problem for years without knowing it. You may have started to rely on prescription drugs to help you get by. And in the midst of your struggle, you look at your children and hope they will have a better life. You want to help them stay off alcohol and drugs. But you can't help kids stay off alcohol and drugs if you are using sleeping pills every night or you are a practicing alcoholic. The strongest message your children hear from you is the message they see and experience. If you have a drug or alcohol problem, we urge you to take care of it as soon as possible.

You may be a heavy drinker and yet not be convinced you have a problem. Your reluctance to help your children might be subconscious because of doubts about yourself.

Five Symptoms to Look for in Identifying an Addict

This whole subject may produce repeated cringes from the guilt you feel about your own drinking or drugging. As many recovering users know, the times of greatest guilt are the times of highest motivation to stop using. The guilt feelings might come after a binge or after bailing a child out of jail for driving while intoxicated. You might have done something that humiliated the family and shattered the image of a family "that has its act together." Perhaps reading this book or experiencing one of those dreadful moments has led you to question whether you have a problem severe enough that it demands you quit. Or perhaps you have been dabbling in drugs, and you want to know if you have become addicted. The following points will help you determine if in fact you have an alcohol or drug problem.

High Tolerance

As we have mentioned before, alcoholics and drug addicts all have one thing in common—the ability to drink or use drugs in large quantities. The large amounts of chemical addicts the body to the point where the cells crave it. What is considered a large amount varies for each person, but you know if you are one of those who can drink more or use more drugs than others can. You have probably passed on to your kids the ability to consume vast quantities of an addictive chemical, making them sitting ducks for the same problem.

A Real Man Knows His Limits

Growing up in Texas, I (Steve) was around many people who took great pride in their abilities to hold liquor. It was not uncommon to attend social functions and watch the men consume beer after beer all day and into the night. These were not drunkards or irresponsible men. They had been raised with the understanding that manhood had something to do with the ability to hold alcohol and maintain control. These people drank this way for most of their lives and produced children who drank that way also.

Not until later in life, because of aging, did their tolerances go down. When their bodies could no longer process the alcohol, their drinking became unpredictable and uncontrollable. Then they were recognized as having a drinking problem. But my Texan friends were alcoholics long before their livers quit working or their drinking went out of control.

If you have a high tolerance for drugs or alcohol, you need to get help. You have become addicted, and that addiction will not go away. It will begin to control you in more painful and obvious ways. The only way to control it is through abstinence.

Compulsion to Use Chemicals Again and Again

The person who has an alcohol or drug problem will consume large amounts and repeat the process again and again. Between times of using alcohol or drugs, the compulsion to use them again controls most if not all thoughts and emotions. The person is obsessed with when and where the next drink or drug will come from. Without the alcohol or drug in the system, the addict feels incomplete. He or she needs the chemical either to feel better or just to feel normal.

Some addicts go for months without using a drug or taking a

drink, and by abstaining that long, they think they are in control. But during those times of restraint, they continually think about what it would be like to drink or use drugs. They "white knuckle" it, hanging on to anything they can that will prevent drug use that day. This can hardly be called "being in control." In fact, the chemical has total control. The compulsion lives and grows inside. Finally it drives them to repeat the act of drinking and using drugs.

Intense Dysphoria

Euphoria is the feeling of intense pleasure. The opposite is dysphoria. People drink or take drugs in search of euphoria. When most people stop, they return to a normal state. But for an addict, there is no return to normal. If they stop consuming alcohol or drugs, they experience severe dysphoria.

Addicts feel intense agony and depression. They have tremendous, uncontrollable mood swings. Thoughts and emotions are extremely hard to bear. They may cry uncontrollably. They may have attempted suicide in times of dark struggles. They feel this way because their nerves are accustomed to the chemical, and without its saturation, their entire psychological economy is distorted. They become emotionally bankrupt. They desperately return to the chemical to ease the pain.

Dysphoria and its consequences have been more fully understood since the crack epidemic swept across our country. This chemical gives an intense high followed by a screeching dysphoria that thrusts the user into deep despair. The user is left craving the drug in an effort to stop the emotional pain. If the user feels worse when not using drugs than when he or she started, the body is addicted. We do not know anyone who can honestly say, "My life is better because of my use of illegal drugs."

Continued Use of Chemicals in the Midst of Adverse Circumstances

When a person watches problems increase all around him or her and still continues the behavior that causes these problems, it's not normal. Family, friends, job, self-esteem, and many other worthwhile things will be destroyed as the person continues to hang on to something that can no longer bring satisfaction. The only reason the person continues using the chemical is that the addiction has him or her hooked. A person would not make a rational decision to destroy his or her life for the sake of a chemical. But because the person is trapped in addiction, he or she continues to use drugs or alcohol no matter how bad life becomes.

When people are addicted, the consequences begin to affect certain areas of their lives, but soon they affect every area. For each person, the order of events may be different, but the adverse consequences are inevitable. Family problems erupt as the drinking and drugging drive family members away, each one feeling betrayed and hurt. Job performance declines. Friends go the other way, repulsed by actions the addict takes under the influence. The irritating effects of the chemicals wear down the body and cause disease. But as tragedy after tragedy piles up, the addict still refuses to make a move toward recovery. This failure occurs not because the person is weak but because of the powerful grip addiction has on the body.

Other People Telling You That You Have a Problem

The strongest indicator of addiction is that others have taken the risk of telling you that your behavior is not normal. They have not done this to hurt you, and they certainly have not done it hastily. They have put off telling you many times and finally could delay no longer. And when you hear of your failures from more than one person, do not think they are conspiring against you. Believe that others care enough to confront you. You have a problem, and you must get help.

An old saying states that if one person calls you a horse, ignore it. If two people call you a horse, ask what they mean. But if three people call you a horse, it is time to saddle up. If these indicators are present in your life, it is time for you to saddle up to the responsibility of doing something about the problem. It is time to get help so you can help your children avoid the pain and suffering you have experienced.

Time to Take Action

If these indicators make you uncomfortable, it is because you can too easily relate to them. Wait no longer. Recovery won't kill you, but the drugs and alcohol will. Make a decision for your own good and contact a professional or call the number in the back of this chapter.

Perhaps these symptoms mentioned don't describe you and your feelings, but they describe your spouse. If you live with an alcoholic or drug addict, you have seen these symptoms develop through the years. Apply to your spouse what you have learned from the chapter on intervention. One of the reasons your children have chosen the way of drugs is that you have not helped stop the progression in your mate. As a result, the kids have modeled the behavior they have seen or used chemicals to escape the pain of the family. Do not wait any longer.

The greatest gift you can give your family is the willingness to struggle through the pain of intervention. When you do, it can be the beginning of a new, successful family and a new life. It is never too late to start.

Drug-proof kids come from drug-free parents. Free yourself and your family. Become willing to do whatever it takes to raise drug-proof children in a drug-saturated society. Life comes with no guarantees, but your actions are the best hope for saving your children from the destruction of alcohol and drugs.

Summary for Drug-Proofing

1. *Education:* Teach your children the facts about alcohol and drug abuse. Ensure that they know the consequences.
2. *Prevention:* Use both positive and negative reinforcements to motivate your children to make the decision to abstain.

3. *Identification:* Learn to identify the signs of drug and alcohol use and abuse. If your children use drugs or alcohol, be the first to know.

4. *Intervention:* If you discover your children have a problem, act now to intervene. Seek help rather than hope or expect the problem to go away.

5. *Treatment:* Find the resources that best fit your situation and uphold the values of your faith and family.

6. *Supportive follow-up:* Prevent relapses by becoming an active participant in your children's recovery.

7. *Self-evaluation:* Examine your own involvement with alcohol and drugs. Solve your problem or at least start a treatment plan before you try to help your children.

If you or your children need help obtaining immediate information or treatment for an alcohol or drug problem, call New Life Ministries toll-free at 1-800-NEW-LIFE.

If you would like more information on "Raising Drug-Proof Kids," a church/small group curriculum in audio and video formats is available from HomeWord. This material is based on the principles outlined in this book. Go to www.HomeWord.com or call 1-800-397-9725.

Discussion Leader's Guide

The following guidelines will help you organize and conduct a discussion series about drug-proofing kids that will benefit any group of parents.

The optimum-size discussion group is 10 to 15 people. A smaller group may decline in interest unless everyone has a high level of commitment. A larger group will require strong leadership skills to help everyone participate meaningfully.

1. If you are leading a group that already meets regularly, such as a Sunday school class, Bible-study group, parent support group, and the like, decide how many weeks to spend on the series, and then set your meeting dates.

   Consider holidays or other events that might affect the continuity of attendance. In most cases, 5 to 10 sessions is a good time period to adequately deal with the major issues in this book.

2. If you want to start a parents' group or bring a group of parents together for the duration of the study, secure several copies of the book to help you enlist two or three parents as a nucleus for the group. Work with these parents to determine the meeting time, dates, and place that are best for your group. Involve this nucleus in inviting other parents to participate.

   Encourage people to register their intention to attend, both to help you in planning and to increase their determination to be there. Follow up with reminder phone calls.

3. Arrange for quality childcare for each session.

4. Plan for light refreshments to be served each session as people arrive to encourage a climate of friendly interchange.

5. Arrange seating informally, either in one semicircle or several smaller circles of no more than eight chairs per circle.

6. At the first session, provide each parent with a copy of this book and a typed schedule for the series.

7. As the leader, briefly share one or two personal ways in which this book has benefited you. This should not be a sales pitch for the book. Just demonstrate honest sharing, being open with the group about your own desire to grow as a person and as a parent. As the discussion leader, you need not be a parenting or drug expert. The group will appreciate your being a fellow learner.

8. In each session, lead group members in discussing the questions for the chapter being considered. If you have more than 8 or 10 parents in your group, assign some of the questions to be discussed in smaller groups. Invite each group to share one or two insights when you congregate back into the larger group.

   Alternate large-group and small-group discussion to provide variety and to allow every group member a comfortable option in which to participate. Try various combinations in forming small groups—couples in separate groups, separate groups for moms and dads, groups based on the number or age of children, and so on.

9. In guiding the discussions, the following tips are helpful:
   - If a question or comment is raised that is off the subject, either suggest that it be dealt with at another time or ask the group if it would prefer to pursue the new issue now.
   - If someone talks too much, direct a few questions specifically to other people, making sure not to put

a shy person on the spot. Talk privately with the "dominator," asking for his or her cooperation in helping elicit comments from a few of the quieter group members.

- If someone does not participate verbally, assign a few questions to be discussed in pairs, groups of three, or other small groups. Or distribute paper and pencils and ask people to write their answers to a specific question or two. Then invite several people, including the "shy" ones, to read what they wrote.

- If someone asks a question and you don't know the answer, admit it and move on. If the question calls for insight about personal experience, invite group members to comment. If the question requires specialized knowledge, offer to look for an answer in the library, from your pastor, or from some other appropriate resource before the next session.

10. Pray regularly for the sessions and the participants. As you guide people in learning from God's Word, He will honor your service and bring rich benefits into the lives of the parents who participate.

Study and Discussion Guide

Chapter 1
"Not My Kid!": Drug Abuse in Your Home

Begin the process of drug-proofing your kids by embracing the truth and moving into action.

Just for Openers

"We had no idea." This response is common when parents find out about their kids' alcohol or drug abuse. How well do you know your child? Respond to the following questions to find out.

> With what two friends does your child spend most of his or her time?

> What kind of influence are the friends on your kid?

For Further Discovery

- What do you know about your kids' friends?

- Have you met their parents? What are their names?

- Do they have brothers and sisters? What are their names?

- Are your kids' friends Christians?

- Are your kids' friends familiar?

- How is your kids' schoolwork?

- What are your kids' interests, dreams, and goals?

- What kinds of music do your kids listen to? What messages does this music communicate?

- What are your kids' attitudes about alcohol and drug use?

- Have your kids ever been offered alcohol or other drugs?

- In what social settings do your kids most often find themselves? Are these settings in which alcohol and drugs are easily accessible?

A Deeper Look

There are four major reasons parents are not making the difference they could.

1. Ignorance.

   On a scale of 1 to 10, with 1 being a little and 10 being a lot, how much do you know about your kids' world?

   1 2 3 4 5 6 7 8 9 10

2. Denial.

   Denial is a common response to kids' use of drugs and alcohol. List as many reasons for denial as you can find in this chapter. Then circle which, if any of these, might be your own response.

3. Guilt.

In what ways does guilt paralyze and stand in the way of change-producing actions?

How have you acted or failed to act when faced with guilt?

4. Fear.

The fear of rejection, the fear of change, and the fear of the unknown can keep parents from taking steps to stop the drug epidemic. What are some other fears parents might have that keep them from action?

Steps for Change

"We loved you so much that we were delighted to share with you not only the gospel of God but our lives as well, because you had become so dear to us" (1 Thessalonians 2:8).

In this passage, Paul suggests two important steps to influence those you love to make God-centered choices. What are those two steps?

Your children are looking for examples to follow. In what ways is the gospel of God fresh and life-changing to you today?

Action

I (Jim) remember the profound influence my dad had on my life when I realized that he read his Bible daily before work. My dad was seeking fresh guidance from the gospel of God.

What are three ways you can make your relationship with God evident to your children?

How can you share, beyond just recounting, what God is doing in your life with your kids this week?

What one thing will you do to get to know your kids better this week?

Chapter 2
The Facts About Drug and Alcohol Abuse

You can drug-proof your kids and alleviate the pressures to use drugs by being a part of the transitional generation.

Just for Openers

Take some time to dream and plan for your kids' future. What do you dream for their lives? When your kids reach the end of life, what do you wish they will say about life?

A Deeper Look

You have learned from the shocking statistics that the problem of drug use is getting worse. The liquor and tobacco industries target the youth of today with thousands of messages to drink, smoke, and chew. What tactics have you observed that confirm this truth?

Steps for Change

"Therefore everyone who hears these words of mine and puts them into practice is like a wise man who built his house on the rock. The rain came down, the streams rose, and the winds blew and beat against that house; yet it did not fall, because it had its foundation on the rock" (Matthew 7:24-25).

Why didn't the house in this Scripture passage fall?

In the passage, Jesus shares His dream and plan for your life. What is it?

Action

On a beach in Baja, Mexico, I (Jim) stood on the edge of a rock that had withstood the ocean's waves for thousands of years. I watched each wave furiously beat against the rock. Though I could feel a slight vibration from the powerful explosion of water against stone, and I caught some of the cool spray on my face as the rock dispersed the impact, I was upright and unharmed. *What if I tried to go against the waves by myself? What if I entered the waters in an attempt to take on life's storms myself?* I wondered. My conclusion was obvious: I would be beat to death. And so will youth without a firm foundation on which to build their futures.

"Drug-proof kids have hope mainly because their parents have made a conscious decision to get involved. Once you have accepted the responsibility to help your children, you are ready to form a plan and carry it out."

Are you willing to commit to taking the responsibility of helping save your kids from the pressures to use drugs?

List five steps in your plan for drug-proofing your children.

With what two people will you share your decision, and when will you share it?

Chapter 3
How Do Kids Become Addicts?

Get a clear understanding of how kids get started misusing drugs and alcohol to prevent your kids from becoming statistics.

Just for Openers

"Kids are living in emotional pain, and they want relief. But instead of finding real relief, they become addicted."

> From what you already know about your kids, your childhood, and the statements made in the book, identify some of the causes of emotional pain for kids today.

> What are two specific circumstances that have caused your kids to feel emotional pain?

A Deeper Look

"Experts estimate that between 85 to 95 percent of teenagers will experiment with alcohol and other drugs."

> There are six major factors that lead kids to drug and alcohol abuse. What are they?

> Of these six, which two most concern you? Why?

Steps for Change

> [10] I rejoice greatly in the Lord that at last you have renewed your concern for me. Indeed, you have been concerned,

but you had no opportunity to show it. [11] I am not saying this because I am in need, for I have learned to be content whatever the circumstances. [12] I know what it is to be in need, and I know what it is to have plenty. I have learned the secret of being content in any and every situation, whether well fed or hungry, whether living in plenty or in want. [13] I can do everything through him who gives me strength. [14] Yet it was good for you to share in my troubles (Philippians 4:10-14).

Paul is walking down memory lane with the Philippians. What does Paul say he has learned and now knows in verses 11 and 12?

According to verse 13, Paul has also learned a life-changing lesson. What is that lesson?

Paul did not always have the confidence in God to help him do all things through Christ's strength—he had to learn it.

Do your children know that they can do all things through Christ? How have you taught, or how can you teach, this lesson?

Action

You can help your kids avoid being part of the 85 percent of kids who experiment with drugs by applying Philippians 4:13 to your parenting skills. Each of the following six factors contain clear "I can" directions your kids need.

1. *Biological predisposition:* "Certain kids get hooked much faster than normal. These kids *must* be told that because

of their family backgrounds, they simply don't have the freedom to experiment....50 percent of the patients come from families where a parent is an alcoholic."

2. *Peer pressure:* "We can't simply assume our children will say no because we told them to do so. We must help them understand the influence their friends have on them. We must build up their self-esteem because kids who have positive self-images have more resistance to peer pressure. And we must take the time to get acquainted with our children's friends."

3. *Parental attitudes:* "The most important influence on a child's attitudes about alcohol and drugs is still the child's parents. Simply put, 'Children see, children do.'...So one of the most important pieces of advice we can give parents is this: 'Don't model alcohol or drug use. Period.'"

4. *Life crisis:* "Like adults, children have to deal with stresses....As with adults, alcohol and drugs can serve to deaden the pain."

5. *Depression:* "A certain amount of depression is normal among teenagers....Boredom is normal for teens, especially in early adolescence, but only for short time periods....Research indicates that children who have low levels of imagination and lack creativity are more readily bored, and these children are more likely to turn to drugs. This is why it is important to encourage children, from a young age, to participate in athletics, drama, dance, music, art, or any other kind of creative activity. If you can keep your children from a crisis of boredom, you can help prevent problems in the future."

6. *Parenting style:* "Mental health professionals are unanimous—children aren't getting enough supervision. Far too many parents have given up on investing the quality and quantity of time it takes to create a loving, firm, and caring environment." Dr. H. Stephen Glenn, former director of the National Drug Abuse Center in Washington, D.C., says, "Children base their behavior on their perception of what is true, not on what is actually

true.... Children are more likely to perceive loving intentions when tone of voice and actions convey dignity and respect along with firmness."

Chapter 4
Cigarettes and Alcohol: The Gateway to Drug Addiction

Take the time to train your children and ensure for them the best chance of not doing drugs or alcohol.

Just for Openers

What are five valuable lessons you learned from a parent or a significant adult in your formative years?

Do you still use those lessons today?

A Deeper Look

"When in doubt, kids imitate what they have seen their parents do. Like it or not, your children are copying your example." It is not common to hear a teen say, "I had to ask myself, What would my mom or dad do if he or she was in this situation?" Keeping this in mind, answer the following questions honestly:

What messages do you communicate through your example to your children about drugs?

Do you have an occasional drink to relax or enhance a social event?

What drugs do you take? For what reasons?

If necessary, are you willing to give these up so your children can be free of drug and alcohol problems?

Steps for Change

"Train a child in the way he should go, and when he is old he will not turn from it" (Proverbs 22:6).

What does this proverb tell a parent he or she is to do?

What are the results of a parent training his or her child?

Action

If I (Steve) ever need to get anywhere in my home state and I'm unsure about just what route to take, I can go to my dad and ask him. My dad has done extensive traveling throughout the Western United States. He can read a map as well as anybody. If I want to go somewhere, he has probably been there, and if not, he knows how to get there. Best of all, he knows the most expedient way to get to my destination, depending on whether I want scenery, speed, or good restaurants along the way. How come my dad knows so much about giving directions? As I stated, my dad has done a lot of traveling, so he knows the best way to get to places.

Your children are asking for direction from you. Many decisions are ahead of your children, and they need direction. If your children don't get it from you, they will go somewhere else. There are three bases for teaching kids about alcohol and drugs. Respond to the questions.

1. *Responsible versus irresponsible behavior.* Do you think you make responsible decisions?

   Do you think you have trained your kids in the art of making responsible decisions?

   What more will you do to train your children to make responsible decisions?

2. *Social and communication skills.* Do you think you communicate your comfortable and uncomfortable feelings clearly, honestly, and openly?

Do you think you have trained your children in the art of social communication through example and exposure to social settings?

What more will you do to train your kids in social communication?

3. *The dangers of losing control.* Do you think you take the time to explain the consequences of the decisions your kids may make, or do you tell them what to do?

Do you think you have trained your kids in the art of identifying the consequences to the decisions they may make?

What more will you do to train your children to identify possible consequences?

Chapters 5 through 8
The Facts About Illicit Drugs

Help your children understand the principle of "What you see is not always what you get."

Just for Openers

Let's play "Name that Drug." A common commercial slogan for a familiar drug is given. Write down the name of the drug.

It soothes and coats your upset stomach.

It is the nighttime sneezing, sniffling, coughing, so-you-can-sleep medicine.

How do you spell relief?

Juan Valdez makes the richest, most aromatic.

With what do your teens "oxycute" their pimples?

Commercials that advertise familiar over-the-counter drugs express a relaxed attitude about drugs. They communicate that we should never have to endure pain or be uncomfortable. This is a fallacy.

A Deeper Look

To be fully equipped to discuss the facts about illicit drugs, complete the following chart.

Drug Name	Why kids like it	How it hurts kids
Tobacco		
Cannabis		
Inhalants		
Cocaine & Crack		
Other Stimulants		
Sedative-hypnotics		
PCP		
LSD		
Mescaline, peyote, psilocybin & other hallucinogens		
Narcotics		
Designer Drugs		

Steps for Change

"Wine is a mocker and beer a brawler; whoever is led astray by them is not wise" (Proverbs 20:1).

Where is a person led by beer and wine?

What does that make such a person?

Why does the decision to turn to a drug make a person unwise?

Action

You've had the opportunity in this chapter to discover the facts about illicit drugs. Now you are equipped to share these facts with your children. Here are some suggestions for sharing.

1. Play the game "drug dictionary." On individual cards, write the names of the drugs you have previously discussed. One by one, each family member chooses a card and reads aloud the word. The rest of the players write down the most creative definition for the word while the player who selected the card writes down the correct definition. After one minute passes, the announcing player collects the cards, shuffles them, and reads aloud the definitions. The group then votes on the most accurate definition of the word. The player(s) who selects the correct definition earns 100 points. Take time to discuss each correct definition and the consequences of the drug's use.

2. Host a drug awareness dessert. Invite many families. Have an informed parent, youth pastor, teacher, or Drug Abuse Resistance Education (DARE) officer present information on illicit drugs and lead a group discussion.

   Remember that opening the line of communication between you and your child is essential to successfully maintaining a drug-free family.

Chapter 9
Roadblocks and Building Blocks

Make a positive difference in your kids' battles against drug use by being an "I can" parent.

Just for Openers

Look at the following two lists and compare them.

1940 Dallas, Texas, study of high school students' biggest problems:
- Running in hallways
- Chewing gum in class
- Wearing improper clothing
- Making noise
- Not putting papers in trash can

1980s Dallas, Texas, study of high school students' biggest problems:
- Robbery
- Assault
- Drug abuse
- Arson
- Bombing
- Alcohol abuse
- Carrying weapons on campus
- Absenteeism
- Vandalism
- Murder
- Extortion

What were the biggest problems you faced as a teenager?

A Deeper Look

"We were never their age." You were 10, 13, 16, 20, and so on, but you were never the age of your children. Today's youth fight what literally seems to be a revolutionary war. Many of these kids are wounded physically, emotionally, and spiritually. Look again through the descriptions of the revolutionary battles your kids face listed in this chapter in the book portion.

> From your perspective, what are the most disturbing facts?

> Now, from your kids' perspectives, what are the most overwhelming facts?

Steps for Change

> According to 1 Samuel 17:34-37,45-47, why did David have an "I can" mind-set?

> What was the outcome of David's stand against the giant?

David could have approached the battle from a different perspective. He could have said, "I can't. I haven't got the time or the resources. I don't understand the big guy over there. I've never been that tall." Fortunately for the children of Israel, David didn't say those negative words. Fortunately for your children, you don't have to say "I can't" either. Just as David chose some small stones that made a big difference, you can choose to make some small changes that will make a big difference in your kids' battles against the giants they face. It may mean some adjusting, but you can do it.

Action

Start now by evaluating yourself on the six building blocks of a solid foundation of growth. In the following list of building blocks, check the box that best describes your effectiveness.

1. Give your children time and attention.

___ *Needs work*   ___ *Doing okay*   ___ *Keep it up*

What is one way you can improve on this building block this week?

2. Give your children integrity.

___ *Needs work*   ___ *Doing okay*   ___ *Keep it up*

What is one way you can improve on this building block this week?

3. Give your children affirmation.

___ *Needs work*   ___ *Doing okay*   ___ *Keep it up*

What is one way you can improve on this building block this week?

4. Give your children opportunities to communicate.

___ *Needs work*   ___ *Doing okay*   ___ *Keep it up*

What is one way you can improve on this building block this week?

5. Give your children a support network.

___ *Needs work*   ___ *Doing okay*   ___ *Keep it up*

What is one way you can improve on this building block this week?

6. Give your children a spiritual foundation.

__ *Needs work*   __ *Doing okay*   __ *Keep it up*

What is one way you can improve on this building block this week?

Chapter 10
Identifying Chemical Abuse in Your Kids

Your children's chances for changed behavior are improved by your ability to detect drug and alcohol use and take positive action.

Just for Openers

Think about your children for a minute.

Do some of your kids' behaviors seem out of the ordinary? What are they?

As objectively as possible, look at each behavior and ask yourself, Do I need to be very concerned about this?

Write down the behaviors that concern you and why they concern you.

A Deeper Look

"There is a large discrepancy between the number of kids who use drugs and the number of parents who think their kids use them.... That is why it is best to look for the problem rather than expect your children will escape using drugs." This chapter presents some generalities about kids who stay sober and symptoms of kids who abuse chemicals.

Think about your children's behaviors in the last 12 months. Now look at the following list and check "Yes" if you have reason for concern and "No" if you don't have reason for concern.

Traits of Sobriety

__ Yes __ No   You are able to communicate with your children

__ Yes __ No   You know and approve of your children's friends

__ Yes __ No   Your children perform adequately and consistently in school

__ Yes __ No   Your kids are involved in healthy activities outside of school

__ Yes __ No   Your children smile, laugh, and are involved with the family

__ Yes __ No   The way your kids dress may not be what you would choose, but the clothing is fairly clean, neat, and free of drug paraphernalia and images

__ Yes __ No   Your children have the ability to say no

__ Yes __ No   Your kids are honest with you

__ Yes __ No   Your children's moods are relatively stable

__ Yes __ No   Your children openly communicate a consistent message that they don't do drugs, their friends don't do drugs, and they disapprove of doing drugs.

Subtle Symptoms of Chemical Abuse

__ Yes __ No   Secrecy

__ Yes __ No   Change in friends

__ Yes __ No   Change in dress and appearance

__ Yes __ No   Increased isolation

__ Yes __ No   Change in interests or activities

__ Yes __ No   Drop in grades

__ Yes __ No   Getting fired from an after-school job

__ Yes __ No   Changes in behavior around the home

__ Yes __ No   Staying out all night

__ Yes __ No   Possession of a bottle of eyedrops (to counter blood-shot eyes)

__ Yes __ No   Sudden change in diet that includes sweets and junk food (many drugs give the users cravings or "munchies")

__ Yes __ No   Dropping out of sports participation

Not-So-Subtle Symptoms of Chemical Abuse

__ Yes __ No   Deep depression accompanied by hours of extra sleep

__ Yes __ No   Depression

__ Yes __ No   Extreme withdrawal from the family

__ Yes __ No   Increased, unexplained absenteeism from school

__ Yes __ No   Little or no involvement in church activities

__ Yes __ No   Increase in mysterious phone calls that produce frantic reactions

__ Yes __ No   Starting smoking

__ Yes __ No   Money problems

__ Yes __ No   Extreme weight loss or gain

__ Yes __ No   Appearance of new friends, older than your child

__ Yes __ No   Expulsion from school

__ Yes __ No   Rebellious and argumentative behavior

__ Yes __ No   Listening to heavy metal rock or rap music with pro-drug lyrics

__ Yes __ No   Acting disconnected or "spacey"

__ Yes __ No   Physically hurting younger siblings

___ Yes ___ No Attempting to change the subject or skirt the issue when asked about drug or alcohol use

___ Yes ___ No Changing the word "party" from a noun to a verb

___ Yes ___ No Discussing times in the future when he or she will be allowed to drink legally

___ Yes ___ No Long periods of time in the bathroom

___ Yes ___ No Burnt holes in clothes or furniture

Surefire Indicators of Chemical Abuse

___ Yes ___ No Paraphernalia found in the bedroom

___ Yes ___ No Possession of large amounts of money

___ Yes ___ No Needle marks on the arms or clothing that prevents you from seeing the arms

___ Yes ___ No Valuables disappearing from the house

___ Yes ___ No Arrests due to alcohol- or drug-related incidents

___ Yes ___ No Repeatedly has bloodshot eyes

___ Yes ___ No Uncontrollable bursts of laughter with no apparent reason

___ Yes ___ No A runny or itchy nose that is not attributable to allergies or a cold (a red nose would also be an indicator)

___ Yes ___ No Dilated or pinpoint pupils

___ Yes ___ No Puffy or droopy eyelids that partially hang over the iris

___ Yes ___ No Mention of suicide or an attempt at suicide

___ Yes ___ No Disappearance or dilution of alcohol in the liquor cabinet

___ Yes ___ No Time spent with people you know use drugs or alcohol

___ Yes ___ No Medicines disappearing from the medicine cabinet

___ Yes ___ No Defending peers' right to use drugs or alcohol

Steps for Change

"Consider it a sheer gift, friends, when tests and challenges come

at you from all sides. You know that under pressure, your faith-life
is forced into the open and shows its true colors. So don't try to
get out of anything prematurely. Let it do its work so you become
mature and well-developed, not deficient in any way. If you don't
know what you're doing, pray to the Father. He loves to help. You'll
get His help, and won't be condescended to when you ask for it"
(James 1:2-5 MSG).

> What is the result of the tests and challenges that assault
> you?

> Eugene Peterson's *The Message* says, "So don't try to get
> out of anything prematurely." What do you think would
> be the result of escaping the steps that face you in drug-
> proofing your kids?

> What can you do when you don't know what to do?

> What is the result?

Action

In the 12 steps to recovery, the first three steps are summed up
by these three statements: Step one is when you admit "I can't."
Step two is when you admit "God can." And step three is when you
decide "I'll let Him." If a person is not able to admit step one completely (which is an admission of powerlessness over situations), it
is impossible to progress to steps two and three. It becomes the constant battle of who knows best, God or me? What you do with the
information in this chapter requires God's guidance. Your action is
simple: Take the time to honestly admit to God that you are powerless in wisdom, confidence, self-control, unconditional love, energy,

or any other area of which you are conscious. You need His guidance and joy to take action. Take the time to pray. God bless you!

Chapter 11
Learning to Intervene

All the horrible consequences of out-of-control addiction can be avoided through the process of intervention.

Just for Openers

> Describe a time in your life when a loved one confronted you in an accurate and constructive way about a behavior.

> What were the consequences of the confrontation?

A Deeper Look

The goal of an intervention is to assist in changing your children's behavior. "Because most change is brought about by a crisis, intervention precipitates a crisis." As I am sure you know by now, alcohol and drug abuse have consequences that affect the whole family. That's why we shared the intervention process as a family experience.

> Answer the following questions to assist you in evaluating what you may need to do to prepare your family for the intervention.

> 1. *Assessment:* "The first step is an assessment of the family by a professional."
>
> Do you have a family counseling therapist?
> ___Yes   ___No

If your answer is no, list five resources you can use to find a therapist for your family.

Do you know of other family members who have been chemically dependent?
___ *Yes*   ___ *No*

If yes, list their names.

2. *Classes:* "The family must then attend classes to become familiar with addiction, codependency, and intervention."

   What can you do today to prepare yourself for attending an Alcoholics Anonymous meeting or other class in your community?

   What are some of your concerns about attending?

The next four steps to intervention are: intervention rehearsal, intervention data, intervention alternatives, and the intervention event. These four steps follow directly after your action on the first two steps.

Make a commitment to take the first two steps.

When will you start the intervention process?

Steps for Change

8"The Amalekites came and attacked the Israelites at Rephidim.

⁹Moses said to Joshua, 'Choose some of our men and go out to fight the Amalekites. Tomorrow I will stand on top of the hill with the staff of God in my hands.' ¹⁰So Joshua fought the Amalekites as Moses had ordered, and Moses, Aaron and Hur went to the top of the hill. ¹¹As long as Moses held up his hands, the Israelites were winning, but whenever he lowered his hands, the Amalekites were winning. ¹²When Moses' hands grew tired, they took a stone and put it under him and he sat on it. Aaron and Hur held his hands up—one on one side, one on the other—so that his hands remained steady till sunset. ¹³So Joshua overcame the Amalekite army with the sword" (Exodus 17:8-13).

When were the Israelites winning?

What two significant things happened in verse 12?

What was the result of Aaron and Hur holding up Moses' hands?

Moses could not have stood strong without the support of two trusted friends. The victory you can celebrate will take a great deal of support from trusted friends who are not directly involved in the intervention themselves.

Action

As you go through the steps we have discussed for intervention, what two friends can you go to for support?

Your own stamina depends on having the necessary support. When will you tell your friends the whole story and ask for their help?

Chapter 12
Getting Help

You can be confident your children will be strengthened and your values supported by following the guidelines in this chapter.

Just for Openers

When obtaining treatment for anything, you have certain criterion you use to make decisions.

> What are some of the components you look for when finding treatment from a doctor, dentist, or medical facility?

> You also may have preconceived ideas about drug treatment centers. What are some of your ideas?

A Deeper Look

"The natural tendency is to try to handle all our problems ourselves, including our children's chemical abuse. But if everything you have tried has failed, it is time to get help. Seeking help is not a sign of weakness but a sign of strength and love....Are you willing to do whatever it takes to help your children recover, to go the extra mile rather than choose what appears to be the easiest path?" These words are difficult truths and challenges, yet you must face them if you really want to see your children get well. If you know what you are looking for from the beginning, you will be able to make the wisest decisions.

> To help you understand the types of available programs, write a description of the types after each title in the following list:

1. Inpatient hospital:

2. Residential treatment:

3. Halfway house:

4. Day treatment:

5. Outpatient care:

Steps for Change

"Make plans by seeking advice; if you wage war, obtain guidance" (Proverbs 20:18).

> What must you seek to make plans? Why?

> As a parent, you probably tend to believe you already know what is best for your family. What does this proverb tell you that you need?

Congratulations! You have already begun to seek advice and obtain guidance by reading this book. Your actions have begun a process of positive change for your family. Keep it up!

Action

It is time to start evaluating treatment centers. Using the following guidelines, fill in the necessary components for you and your children.

1. For the facility to be a well-maintained facility, it must have:

2. The centers I am looking at were referred to me by:

> Do I trust their opinions?

3. Do I know someone who has been through this center's program?

What was his or her experience?

4. What guidelines does the facility have to support a sober lifestyle in relation to:

Music

Movies

Language

View of sex

5. How does the program staff handle personal attention?

Do they provide one-on-one counseling sessions through-out treatment?

6. Do they have programs for family treatment? What are they?

Do you consider them fruitful for your family?

7. What are the people on staff's attitudes, sensitivity, and service?

8. Is the center sensitive to your personal values?

9. What are some other concerns you might have?

10. Based on your responses, which center and program sounds best for you?

Chapter 13
Parents' Guide to Handling Relapse

Help prevent a relapse or redeem a relapse by understanding what a good recovery plan includes and how to use it.

Just for Openers

Habits of any kind are hard to break. Statistics say it takes about 90 days of practicing a new behavior to make it a habit.

> Have you overcome a habit through discipline and failure and discipline again? What was the habit, and with what behavior did you replace it?

A Deeper Look

"Good coaches prepare a team for the struggle ahead. They practice game-like situations so team members will be fully prepared. And good coaches develop a plan they will follow during the competition. But the best coaches always go a step further. They also prepare the team for setbacks so the players know what to do if the other team scores first." A good recovery plan is: 1) a lifelong plan, 2) a family plan, 3) a plan for success, and 4) a realistic plan. Seriously consider the following questions to prepare a plan for yourself.

1. Seeing your addicted child's recovery plan as a lifelong plan can cause a variety of emotional responses. What do you think will be the most common emotional responses for you?

2. A successful recovery plan is a family plan. Do you foresee any potential conflicts to this being true for your family?

3. A good recovery plan is a plan for success. What can you do in advance to ensure the most success from your children's recovery plan?

4. A realistic plan is a wholesome plan. What elements do you think might be introduced into your family's recovery plan that could make it unrealistic?

Steps for Change

"Summing it all up, friends, I'd say you'll do best by filling your minds and meditating on things true, noble, reputable, authentic, compelling, gracious—the best, not the worst; the beautiful, not the ugly; things to praise, not things to curse" (Philippians 4:8 MSG).

With what does Paul tell you to fill your mind? Why?

If you are taking Paul's advice, what influence do you think that will have on your attitude?

If you are taking Paul's advice, what influence do you think that will have on the attitudes of your family?

Action

A young friend of mine (Steve) who completed a 10-day treatment program for cocaine addiction was told that 90 percent of the addicts who come for cocaine treatment will use it again. Unfortunately, nearly a year to the date of his graduation from the program, he did use cocaine again. It is common for some addicts to return to treatment many times until they have mastered the combination for complete recovery. Recovered addicts attribute their successes to the heroes in their lives who loved them enough to be tough. You can be your kids' hero by walking through the recovery plan with them. Consider how you can be a part of the following specific action steps.

1. *Physical:* "Eating habits need to change to ensure that the body can recover strength and rebuild damaged tissue."

   What steps can you take to ensure your family gets a balanced diet?

   - *Exercise:* "Exercise offers tremendous recovery benefits."

     What steps can you take to ensure your family gets more exercise?

   - *Rest and relaxation:* "The body needs plenty of rest, especially in the early stages of recovery."

What steps can you take to ensure your family gets the proper amount of rest?

2. *Mental:* "Addicts need to experience new and powerful information about recovery."

   What steps can you take to ensure your children get the healthiest input and attend the proper lectures and meetings?

3. *Emotional:* "Give your kids experiences at home and in groups of recovering people where feelings can be identified, expressed, and managed."

   What steps can you take to ensure your kids learn how to identify and express feelings in a safe environment?

4. *Social:* "Changing playmates and playgrounds."

   What steps can you take to provide positive social experiences for your kids?

5. *Spiritual:* "Recovery is first and foremost a spiritual process.... As a parent, you can set the pattern for spiritual growth."

   What steps can you take to set a healthy tone for spiritual growth for your family?

Chapter 14
Preventing Drug and Alcohol Abuse: Parents Set the Tone

By your actions, you can help your children avoid a multitude of problems while giving them a future full of choices.

Just for Openers

Take 30 seconds to write down the titles of the five best sermons you have ever heard. Go!

Take 30 seconds to write down the names of the five most influential people in your life. Go!

Which was easiest to remember, the sermons or the people?

A Deeper Look

"As we've said before, your example is the most important tool for preventing your children from using drugs and alcohol." Nine prevention tools are revealed in this chapter. Although all nine tools are important, the success of the final seven rests in what you choose to do with the first two. It is like a math equation: You + God = the final seven prevention tools. For example, your ability to love unconditionally is founded in your ability to develop unconditional love from an intimate relationship with God through Jesus Christ.

Look at the list of the final seven tools and ask yourself, Have I done the best I can? Have I allowed God to lead me as I approach each of these issues in relation to my life? To my family members' lives?

3. Unconditional love?   __ Yes __ No

4. Behavior and discipline? __ Yes __ No

5. Control?   __ Yes __ No

6. Contracts?   __ Yes __ No

7. Friends?   __ Yes __ No

8. Coping?   __ Yes __ No

9. Pressure?   __ Yes __ No

Steps for Change

"Don't be misled: No one makes a fool of God. What a person plants, he will harvest. The person who plants selfishness, ignoring the needs of others—ignoring God!—harvests a crop of weeds. All he'll have to show for his life is weeds! But the one who plants in response to God, letting God's Spirit do the growth work in him, harvests a crop of real life, eternal life. So let's not allow ourselves to get fatigued doing good. At the right time we will harvest a good crop if we don't give up, or quit. Right now, therefore, every time we get the chance, let us work for the benefit of all, starting with the people closest to us in the community of faith" (Galatians 6:7-10 MSG).

What does this passage say a person will harvest?

How does a person harvest a good crop?

What harvest are you reaping with your family right now?

Action

The time is now to look long and hard at that equation: You + God = the final seven prevention tools.

What specific changes do you need to make to implement these tools?

Every recovery program includes God in the first three steps. Have you allowed yourself to fall away from God, the power source in your life?

Has your love for God grown cold?

Are you too busy to keep the fire going in your relationship with God?

Romans 8:35 states that nothing can separate you from the love of God. Though you can easily feel as if God is a billion miles away, He is not. You can renew your relationship with God right now.

First: In prayer, recommit your life into His hands and plans.

Second: Find a friend with whom you can be open about your decision, and ask the friend to hold you accountable for the decision you made to God.

Third: Daily invite God into every aspect of your life, especially when it comes to parenting with the final seven prevention tools.

Where are you in your relationship with God?

You can begin anew today. God bless you!

Chapter 15
Motivating Others to Drug-Proof Their Kids

Help change the lives of thousands of young people and save a community by looking for ways to stop chemical abuse.

Just for Openers

Think about some of the great movements in the past that made a positive difference in the world.

What movement really impressed you?

What person or people were at the heart of that movement?

A Deeper Look

One time we took our youth group on a rock-climbing adventure. The Wednesday before we left on the trip, I (Jim) told our kids, "The most important key to a successful rock-climbing experience is showing up. If you are not on the bus when we leave the parking lot, chances are good that you are not going to have a very good climb." We state in the book text that it is time parents stop pointing fingers and start showing up by looking for ways to make their communities drug-free.

Dream of a community that is drug-free. What is it like?

Who would benefit from a drug-free community?

What five actions can you take that would start or result in a drug-free community?

Who are three people with whom you could take these steps?

Steps for Change

"Let us not become weary in doing good, for at the proper time we will reap a harvest if we do not give up. Therefore, as we have opportunity, let us do good to all people, especially to those who belong to the family of believers" (Galatians 6:9-10).

What does Paul say will happen if you do not give up?

To whom are you to do good?

264   How to Talk to Your Kids About Drugs

What an incredible act of obedience when you follow Paul's instructions and do something good that will be beneficial for many people.

> What can you do today to ensure the longevity of your commitment to do good?

Action

Imagine the incredible difference you can make if you decide to show up and get busy. You can:

- Form a community advisory board
- Lobby at the city council
- Ensure existing laws are strictly enforced in the community
- Form intervention groups on school campuses
- Organize innovative drug education programs
- Start an accountability group for parents
- Provide guidance to parents who struggle with their kids using drugs
- Begin a students-against-drugs group
- Get further training for the purpose of training others

Now for your ideas:

> What else can you do?

Chapter 16
It's Never Too Late to Begin

Make a huge difference in your life and the lives of others by moving into action now.

Just for Openers

Think back over all the information covered in this book.

What fact or thought is most important to you?

What feelings does that thought provoke?

A Deeper Look

The terrible effects of drug use comes down to one choice: "The alternative to acting, however, is to do nothing—a choice full of misery for yourself and those you could help." People allow themselves to believe that the misery they feel as a result of drug use is not as bad as the embarrassment or guilt of coming clean.

What reasons keep you from helping yourself or helping a loved one?

Look closely at the reasons you wrote down. Weigh them against a life of hope, joy, peace, and sobriety.

Which honestly is the better choice?

Steps for Change

" 'For I know the plans I have for you,' declares the LORD, 'plans to prosper you and not to harm you, plans to give you hope and a future. Then you will call upon me and come and pray to me, and I will listen to you. You will seek me and find me when you seek me with all your heart. I will be found by you,' declares the LORD, 'and will bring you back...to the place from which I carried you'" (Jeremiah 29:11-14).

What kind of plans does the Lord have for you?

When does He promise to listen to you?

When will He be found by you?

What will be the result of being found by Him?

Action

Take a survey of the following list of points to determine if you may have an addiction problem. It is time to be honest with yourself.

1. *High tolerance:* Do you have the ability to drink heavily or use a lot of drugs?

2. *Compulsion to use chemicals again and again:* Do you consume large amounts of alcohol or other drugs again and again?

3. *Intense dysphoria:* When you stop drugging or drinking, do you fall into a depression or experience intense mood swings?

4. *Continued use of chemicals in the midst of adverse circumstances:* No matter how bad the consequences get, do you continue to use drugs and drink alcohol?

5. *Other people telling you that you have a problem:* Have others taken the risk of telling you that your behavior is not normal?

The only person who can help you is you. Your decision to

be honest and admit to yourself that you have a chemical abuse problem can make a world of difference in your life and in the lives of your loved ones.

What will you do with the information you learned from this last chapter?

When will you act upon it?

To whom will you tell your discoveries?

The "Just Say No" Game

One way to enhance kids' abilities to withstand pressure is through this game. Used in your family or with a youth group, it teaches refusal techniques. Its best use is between a parent and a child, going over each pressure situation and talking it through.

The object of the game is to respond to a high-pressure situation in such a way that those applying the pressure will back off yet not be antagonized so the situation won't escalate. Work with your child to develop several creative ways to say no to each scenario. And don't be afraid to use humor. Sometimes that's the best way to defuse a situation.

Drug Offers

1. You are at school in between classes, and someone asks you to walk into the bathroom to smoke a joint.

2. A boy you know says he snuck two of his mother's tranquilizers out of the medicine cabinet. He asks you to meet him after school to take them.

3. One of the high school seniors offers to give you a ride home and tells you he has some pure and expensive crack.

4. At one of the local hangouts, a girl offers you a red pill and promises it will make you feel as though you are in another world.

5. You see a friend under the football stadium shooting something into his arm. He offers to let you try it free.

6. On the way to the movies, someone in the car pulls out a handful of pills for everyone to try. He insists that all participate.

7. Your date lights up a joint.

8. At a slumber party, one of the kids starts handing out sleeping pills from her parents' medicine cabinet.

9. You open your notebook in class and find a small envelope with a red pill in it. You look up, and a boy you know is winking at you. He takes a pill like the one you have and puts it in his mouth.

10. Before a basketball game, one of the guys on the team says he has pills to give everyone super energy so the team can win.

11. On the way home from a movie, while stopped at a traffic light, someone comes to the car window and offers you some crack for $10.

12. At a party, a girl pulls out of her purse a razor blade, a mirror, and a vial of cocaine. She puts out "a line," and the entire party is watching as she offers you first "taste."

13. A guy you know is walking with you to see a friend. He pulls from his pocket a cigarette that he says is dusted with PCP. He says that the one he smoked yesterday was wonderful.

14. A girl at a party goes into the kitchen to bake some brownies. A rumor circulates that one of the ingredients is marijuana. She offers you the first sample.

Alcohol Offers

1. Your older brother and his friend pick you up from a party, and his friend offers you a cold beer for the trip home.

2. At a party, the gang gets into the parents' liquor cabinet. Everyone starts drinking out of the bottle of vodka.

3. Your parents take you out to a nice dinner at a local club. Your dad orders something to drink for everyone and tells you it is okay for you to have one.

4. On the drive home from school, one of the people you consider your friend pulls out a bottle of champagne and pops the cork. He tells you to drink up.

5. On a fishing trip, you go up the river with your sister. You are in the middle of the forest, and she says that because no one is around you can have a beer.

6. You want to get into this secret club. At the initiation ceremony, the leader hands you a quart bottle of beer and tells you that to be part of the club, you must drink it.

7. Your friend's dad is offering all of the kids at the party a beer to loosen up.

8. At a local restaurant, the waiter pours a glass of wine for you by mistake.

9. Behind a shed in the vacant lot near your house, you and a friend find a six-pack of beer that is still cold. Your friend suggests the two of you drink it all.

10. You are on a trip to Hawaii, and the flight attendant offers you the same rum punch all the other passengers are drinking.

11. At church camp, one of the counselors, who seems to like you, asks you to meet him outside the bunkhouse when lights go out. You go, thinking it will be a special project or a joke on someone. When you get there, you see he has a bottle in his hand and smells like alcohol. He asks you if you would like some liquor.

12. You get invited to a party of older kids. You are told that everyone will be there, including a celebrity from Hollywood. To entice you to come, the person inviting you tells you everyone will be drinking.

13. On the way home from school, your friend's father begins to drink while he is driving.

14. On a ski trip to the lake, your older cousin takes you out in the boat to the middle of the lake. When you get there, he opens a silver flask full of bourbon and says to take a drink. When you hesitate, he insists it won't hurt you and asks if you're just a big baby.

15. At a local club, to get beer you need to have a stamp on your hand. A friend of yours tells you to meet him at 7:00 in front of the club. He says he can get your hand stamped so you can drink.

16. At a Sunday brunch, the waiter pours some champagne for everyone, including you. Your sister looks at you and says to take a drink because the alcohol is included in the price of the meal.

Notes

Chapter 1—"Not My Kid!"

1. Maia Szalavitz, "Underage Drinking," *STATS at George Mason University,* http://www.alcoholnews.org/underage_drink.html, April 29, 2005.

2. "Troubling Teen Drug Use Statistics," http://www.teendrugabuse.us/teen drugstatistics.html, October 9, 2006.

3. "How Many Teens Use Marijuana?" *National Institute on Drug Abuse for Teens,* http://teens.drugabuse.gov/facts/facts_mj1.asp, October 9, 2006.

4. "Troubling Teen Drug Use Statistics."

5. "How Many Teens Use Marijuana?"

6. National Institute on Drug Abuse, "NIDA InfoFacts: Crack and Cocaine," http://www.drugabuse.gov/Infofacts/cocaine.html, October 30, 2006.

7. CASA, *"So Help Me God: Substance Abuse, Religion and Spirituality,"* November 2001, http://www.TheAntiDrug.com/Faith, October 30, 2006.

Chapter 2—The Facts About Drug and Alcohol Abuse

1. "The 5 Most Expensive Addictions," *Forbes,* http://articles.moneycentral. msn.com/Investing/Forbes/The5MostExpensiveAddictions.aspx, October 13, 2006.

2. "Youth, Alcohol and Drugs: An Overview," National Council on Alcoholism and Drug Dependence, http://www.ncadd.org/facts/youthalc.html, October 30, 2006.

3. Http://www.ncadd.org/facts/youthalc.html, December 14, 2006.

4. Ibid.

5. "The Bottom Line on Alcohol in Society," *Alcohol Research Information Service* 8, no. 4 (Winter 1988): 11.

6. Office of the Inspector General, U.S. Department of Health and Human Services, Youth and Alcohol: A National Survey, "Drinking Habits, Access, Attitudes and Knowledge," Washington, D.C., 1991, p. 6.

7. Maia Szalavitz, "Alcohol and Advertising," *STATS at George Mason University,* http://alcoholnews.org/advertising.html, October 21, 2005.

Chapter 3—How Do Kids Become Addicts?

1. Barbara R. Lorch and Robert H. Hughes, "Church Youth, Alcohol and Drug Education Programs and Youth Substance Use," *Journal of Alcohol and Drug Education* 33, no. 2 (Winter 1988): 15.

2. Ross Campbell, M.D., *Your Child and Drugs* (Wheaton, IL: Victor Books, 1988), pp. 70-71.

3. Ibid.

4. John Q. Baucom, Ph.D., *Help Your Children Say No to Drugs* (Grand Rapids: Zondervan Publishing House, 1987), pp. 130-31.

5. H. Stephen Glenn and Jane Nelsen, *Raising Children for Success: Blueprints & Building Blocks for Developing Capable People* (Fair Oaks, CA: Sunrise Press, 1987), p. 183.

6. Excerpted from Dennis Nelson, "Frequently-Seen Stages in Adolescent Chemical Use" chart (Minneapolis: CompCare Publishers). Used by permission.

Chapter 4—Cigarettes and Alcohol

1. John Q. Baucom, Ph.D., *Help Your Children Say No to Drugs* (Grand Rapids: Zondervan Publishing House, 1987), p. 34.

2. National Institute on Drug Abuse, http://teens.drugabuse.gov/facts/facts nictoine1.asp, October 9, 2006.

3. Centers for Disease Control and Prevention, "Fast Facts," http://www.cdc. gov/tobacco/overview/Facts/Fast_Facts.htm, *Tobacco Information and Prevention Source (TIPS),* March 2006.

4. Centers for Disease Control and Prevention, "About Us," http://www.cdc. gov/tobacco/issue.htm, *Tobacco Information and Prevention Source (TIPS),* October 9, 2006.

5. Alan Bash, "Young smokers more likely to use drugs," *USA TODAY,* October 25, 1993.

6. Centers for Disease Control and Prevention, "Targeting Tobacco Use: The

Nation's Leading Cause of Death," http://www.cdc.gov/nccdphp/publica
tions/aag/osh.htm, October 9, 2006.

7. National Institute on Drug Abuse, "NIDA InfoFacts: Cigarettes and Other
Tobacco Products," http://www.drugabuse.gov/Infofacts/tobacco.html,
October 9, 2006.

8. John DiConsiglio, "Smoking Gun: Three Teens Speak Out," adapted from
Heads Up: Real News About Drugs and Your Body (New York: Scholastic, Inc.,
2003), http://teens.drugabuse.gov/stories/story_nic1.asp, October 9, 2006.

9. Retrieved from http://www.stopalcoholabuse.gov/, October 30, 2006.

10. Maia Szalavitz, "Underage Drinking," *STATS at George Mason University*,
http://www.alcoholnews.org/underagedrink.html, April 29, 2005.

11. For a more detailed explanation of alcoholism, see *Growing Up Addicted* by
Stephen Arterburn (New York: Ballantine Books, 1987).

Chapter 5—Marijuana and Prescription Narcotics

1. National Drug Threat Assessment 2006, http://www.dea.gov/concern/18862/
appendb.htm.

2. Ibid.

3. Ibid.

Chapter 6—Inhalants and Over-the-Counter Drugs

1. "What Every Parent Needs to Know About Cough Medicine," The
Partnership for a Drug-Free America, http://www.drugfree.org/Parent/
Resources/Cough_Medicine_Abuse, September 27, 2006. Check out http://
www.drugfree.org for more information.

2. NIDA InfoFacts: Inhalants, http://www.drugabuse.gov/Infofacts/inhalants.
html, October 9, 2006.

3. Margaret Wagner, "Keith's Law," The Partnership for a Drug-Free America,
http://www.drugfree.org/Portal/memorials/Keiths_Law, November 20, 2006.

Chapter 8—Steroids, Diet Pills, HIV and AIDS

1. Http://www.bodybuilding.com/store/SI/blaze.html, December 14, 2006.

2. Http://www.vanderbilt.edu/AnS/psychology/health_psychology/Eph
edrine_wtloss.htm, December 14, 2006.

3. Cate Baily, "Behind the Bulk: Craig's Story," adapted from *Heads Up: Real
News About Drugs and Your Body* (New York: Scholastic, Inc., 2003), http://
teens.drugabuse.gov/stories/story_ster1.asp, October 9, 2006.

4. Ibid.

5. NIDA InfoFacts: Drug Abuse and AIDS, http://www.drugabuse.gov/Info Facts/DrugAbuse.html, October 9, 2006.

6. National Institute on Drug Abuse, "What Are HIV and AIDS?" http://teens. drugabuse.gov/facts/facts_hiv1.asp, October 9, 2006.

Chapter 9—Roadblocks and Building Blocks

1. U.S. Bureau of the Census, *U.S. Bureau of the Census Statistical Abstract of the United States: 2000.*

2. Maia Szalavitz, "Underage Drinking," *STATS at George Mason University,* http://www.alcoholnews.org/underagedrink.html, April 29, 2005.

3. "Monitoring the Future" Study, 2000 data, Institute for Social Research, University of Michigan, www.monitoringthefuture.org.

4. Department of Education, *What Works: Schools Without Drugs,* Washington, D.C., 1987, p. 15.

5. Steve Arterburn, *Growing Up Addicted,* audiocassette (San Clemente, CA: National Institute of Youth Ministry, 1994).

6. "Teens Drink More Than Parents Think," survey taken during Alcoholism and Drug Abuse Week, July 8, 1992, p. 6.

7. Ray Johnston, *Developing Leadership Potential in Students,* audiocassette of lecture by Ray Johnston at the National Youth Workers Convention, Chicago, 1994.

8. "The New Dads," *BusinessWeek Online,* http://www.businessweek.com/mag azine/content/04_45/b3907122.htm?chan=search, November 8, 2004.

9. David Elkind, *The Hurried Child: Growing Up Too Fast Too Soon* (Cambridge, MA: Perseus Books Group, 2001), p. 138.

10. H. Stephen Glenn, *Developing Capable Young People,* audiocassette (El Cajon, CA: Youth Specialties, 1988).

Chapter 10—Identifying Chemical Abuse in Your Kids

1. HomeWord website, www.homeword.com, November 2006.

Chapter 14—Preventing Drug and Alcohol Abuse

1. CASA, *"So Help Me God: Substance Abuse, Religion and Spirituality,"* November 2001, http://www.TheAntiDrug.com/Faith, October 30, 2006.

Chapter 15—Motivating Others to Drug-Proof Their Kids

1. Vernon J. Bittner, "12 Steps for Christian Living," retrieved from the HomeWord website, www.homeword.com, November 2006.

For more information on drug-proofing your kids, raising children, and marriage improvement resources, you can contact the authors and their ministries.

Contact Stephen Arterburn and/or his ministry:

New Life Ministries
PO Box 1018
Laguna Beach, CA 92652

Counseling & Customer Service
Phone: 1-800-NEW-LIFE (639-5433)
Fax: 1-469-241-6795
www.newlife.com

Contact Jim Burns and/or his ministry:

HomeWord
PO Box 1600
San Juan Capistrano, CA 92693
Phone: 1-800-397-9725
www.homeword.com

Great Resources for Parents from Harvest House Publishers

GOT TEENS?
Time-Tested Answers for Moms of Teens and Tweens
Jill Savage and *Pam Farrel*

Jill Savage, founder of Hearts at Home Ministries, and Pam Farrel, cofounder of Masterful Living Ministries, can shout "Yes!" to the question, "Got Teens?" Now they have teamed up to share their wealth of wisdom (and empathy). Moms don't have to be perfect...just equipped with practical, biblical tools to...

- identify and develop their kids' strengths
- make choices over what kids can do, and who with
- teach manners, compassion, and social responsibility
- guide relationships with the opposite sex
- turn around destructive behavior and bad habits

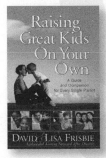

RAISING GREAT KIDS ON YOUR OWN
A Guide and Companion for Every Single Parent
David and *Lisa Frisbie*

In two decades as family counselors, David and Lisa Frisbie have talked to thousands of single moms and dads. They know what you're going through, and they provide practical and proactive ideas you can use to...

- guide your kids through the hurt and pain that follow divorce
- take care of yourself so you can take care of your children
- build strong connections with family and friends and find support through them
- manage your household confidently as you take on new roles and tasks
- make good decisions about work, education, and relationships

In *Raising Great Kids on Your Own*, effective strategies come to life through the Frisbies' candid conversations with moms and dads who parent alone. Their stories—true stories of the good and the bad, of hope and encouragement—will help you raise your kids with optimism and confidence.

LIVING WELL AS A SINGLE MOM
A Practical Guide to Managing Your Money, Your Kids, and Your Personal Life
Cynthia Yates

Life as a single mom may not be what you expected. Still, God's plan of hope for your family hasn't changed. Your number one priority also hasn't changed: to live well so you can help your kids live happy, successful lives.

Once a single mom herself, Cynthia Yates passionately wants you to do just that—with your relationship with God growing, your finances in order, and a team of friends and family ready to help. With straight talk, plenty of humor, and tons of compassion, she will guide you along your journey to living well as a single mom.

WHEN YOUR TEEN IS STRUGGLING
Real Hope and Practical Help for Parents Today
Mark Gregston

When you've tried everything you know to do, Mark Gregston offers this encouragement: Don't lose hope. From his 30-plus years of working with troubled teens, Mark shows you how to help kids work through their pain so they can enjoy the lives God created them to live. With this comprehensive guide, you can...

- develop a belief system your family can live by
- deal with the real issues causing your teens' troublesome behaviors
- build healthy family relationships even in difficult times

> *"Mark shares his secrets to survival and success in raising teenagers, offering parents a hand as they struggle for help. As a parent myself, I say it's about time!"*
> ~ **Steve Largent** ~

MYSPACE®, MYKIDS
A Parent's Guide to Protecting Your Kids and
Navigating MySpace.com
Jason Illian

MySpace, the second-most visited site on the Internet, has more than 100 million users. Chances are your teens are among them. Would you like to know what your kids are posting for the entire world to see? Are you curious about whom your kids are hanging out with online?

Even if you don't have great computer skills, Jason Illian empowers you to understand the benefits and dangers of MySpace and connect with your kids in this new and important way. Now you and your teens can work together to...

- understand what the world of MySpace is all about and what it means to your teens
- avoid leaving "virtual footprints" that online predators could follow
- block unwanted, inappropriate online comments and pictures from others
- develop a family computer policy that facilitates appropriate parental supervision

WHEN GOOD KIDS MAKE BAD CHOICES
Help and Hope for Hurting Parents
Elyse Fitzpatrick and *James Newheiser* with *Dr. Laura Hendrickson*

Authors Elyse Fitzpatrick and Jim Newheiser speak from years of personal experience as both parents and biblical counselors to guide you in how to deal with the emotional trauma that results when a child goes astray. They offer solid hope and encouragement, along with positive steps you can take in even the most negative situations.

Helpful advice from Dr. Laura Hendrickson regarding drugs commonly prescribed to problem children—along with suggested questions you can ask pediatricians about behavioral medications—round out this compassionate, practical guide.

THE MOM I WANT TO BE
Rising Above Your Past to Give Your Kids
a Great Future
T. Suzanne Eller

Your experiences as a mother and a woman are influenced by the mothering you received as a child. Suzie Eller gently, compassionately gives you a healthy vision of the wonderful thing motherhood can be. Drawing from overcoming her own difficult growing-up years, she shows you...

- how shattered legacies can be put back together
- ways to forgive, let go, and leave your parenting baggage in the past
- how to give your kids the gifts of good memories and a great futures

PARENTING: DON'T TRY THIS AT HOME
What I Learned While My Kids Were Raising Me
Phil Callaway

Author and award-winning columnist Phil Callaway captures the amusing and bemusing experiences of the roller-coaster ride called "parenting." In this sparkling collection of stories, you'll recognize those you love...as well as yourself! And the comedy and humanity Phil finds in family life will encourage you—whatever stage you're at in the game—to take notice of each day's gifts of humor and faith.

"This is a book you'll love."
~ **Max Lucado** ~

HARVEST HOUSE
PUBLISHERS